HUBERT MURPHY, JR.

A
BEAUTIFUL
DEATH

*What Life Without
God Really Offers*

A Beautiful Death – What Life Without God Really Offers

Published by E Squared Publishing Group, a Cortney Sargent company.
E Squared Publishing Group
www.esquaredpublishing.net

ISBN-13: 978-0-692-96750-8
Printed in the United States of America.

CONTENTS

Acknowledgements

I would like to acknowledge my high school English teacher, Mrs. Lillian Hollins, for her valuable editorial input on my initial manuscript. Also her husband, Mr. Howard Hollins, for making sure she received all the material I sent. Marilyn Gibbs, who worked diligently on the back cover. To my wonderful family and to the many friends who encouraged me to write this book and supported my effort, our support was greatly needed and appreciated.

HUBERT MURPHY, JR.

Dedication to Pamela

I dedicate this book to my sister Pamela Toombs, who lost her battle with breast cancer. She may have lost the battle, but she fought it with dignity and grace. She fought it with patience and perseverance. She fought it with humility and never once asked "why me?" She fought it for her family. She fought it for her self-respect. She fought it with the same tenacity she used to whip the bigger girl who tried to pick on her in middle school. She was small but she could pack a punch. She was always willing to be a friend in time of need. She gave so much of herself and asked for little in return. She was our guardian angel and a truly special gift. You never know the true value of someone until they are gone. Although I loved her dearly and hated to say goodbye. I knew God loved her more and she was merely going home. I cherish the memories like the time she tried to teach me how to dance -which was a tremendous undertaking since I am quite tall. I wish I had paid more attention to our dance lessons. The scriptures declare, "Be careful to entertain strangers for some have entertained angels unawares" (Hebrews 13:2). My sister Pamela was an angel to me. I will always remember you kiddo, and you will never depart from my heart.

PREFACE

I am writing this book with the intent of providing a down to Earth approach for people seeking answers to some of the hard questions regarding Christianity. Although Christendom is my intended audience, I hope it finds a broader appeal. Perhaps you may be new to Christianity or have become somewhat disillusioned with religion. If you think some of the points are valid for your life, feel free to explore them. I would like to make it known from the beginning I am not an academically trained Bible scholar or philosopher. I am just a common man using mere common sense. Although I happen to be an ordained Baptist minister, I have never considered myself to be religious. Religion restricts you and may cause you to fight your fellow man over something like sprinkling people in water or fully submersing them. While I have been a member of various denominational churches, I have not found much difference in people. Church philosophy, maybe, but not people. I do not mean to stir up any great philosophical or theological debates. I know full well how divisive religion can be, just as I know there is nothing more dangerous than a misguided individual who thinks he is doing something for God.

Whether you are a Christian or someone on their journey to find God, you will surely be bombarded with tough questions and might struggle at first to find a response. That is okay— no one knows everything. I might also add some people will make statements about the Christian faith knowing full well they have already been discredited. They are hoping you do not know what their up to. As I make my points, I will stress that I am not a theologian and refer you to sources that have a broader knowledge of different subject matters. These will include notable writers such as the late C.S. Lewis, a renowned scholar whose storytelling ability is second to none. His *Chronicles of Narnia* series continue to find new audiences generation after generation. As well as current theologians as Professor John Lennox, Ravi Zacharias, William Lane Craig, and Lee Strobel just to name a few. These men are by far the leading Christian voices today and well respected in the realm of Christian apologetics. When I say "apologetics", I am simply referring to the ability to defend the Christian faith and worldview–hopefully in a compassionate and intelligent manner.

I will intentionally avoid attaching any political ideologies to the gospel. I believe that life and teachings of Christ should stand alone, because when you attach political ideologies to the gospel you may run the risk of turning someone away from the beauty of Christ and the love of God. Besides, Jesus did not let himself be dragged into politics, when some attempted, he said render to Caesar the things that are Caesar's and to God the things that are God's (Mark 12:17). Besides I truly hate when people try and tell me how to think, I have never relinquished that right, neither should you. The focus should always remain on the life and teachings of Jesus, not on anything else. I do not know about you, but I have seen far too many so called Christians who claimed God favored their cause, only to find out behind closed doors their conduct was worse than that of so called unbelievers.

I also will not shy away from the arguments against existence of God, the Christian faith, and the utter disdain some people have for religion. I fully acknowledge some arguments against religion are valid. Christianity certainly has its history of abuse and violence, so skepticism is indeed necessary. It is my belief that a religious worldview must be able to stand in the face of criticism if it wants to be taken seriously. Some religions do not even allow honest dialogue. If a so-called religion cannot be criticized, it should not be trusted. We should all be leery of person who gets mad if you ask hard questions. Is it not the goal of honest dialogue to seek the truth and follow the evidence wherever it may lead? This is also where I feel Christianity has an advantage over other religions—it invites you to criticize it.

I will be presenting arguments against the Christian faith from atheists such as Professor Richard Dawkins, Samuel Harris, and Lawrence Krauss to name a few who have branded themselves as the new atheists. Atheism is really nothing new. The new atheists just take a more aggressive tone in their criticism of religion and people who believe in God. This book is in no way an attempt to badger, condemn, or belittle anyone. It is my endeavor to bolster your faith in God and if you do not believe in God, simply peak your interest and curiosity enough to give serious thought to the views I have presented. Having read numerous books by different philosophers as well as listened to countless lectures. There were times I would listen to some scholar or read something and find myself confused.

Obviously, some people are very smart but they lack the ability to communicate effectively. So I will not try to present information that is over your heads but I will not treat you as children either. This book is written as an admonishment to wise living, like King Solomon passing on his wisdom to those who will come after him in the books of Ecclesiastes and Proverbs. Ecclesiastes being one of my favorites, I read it when I was younger and its wisdom has been my constant companion. Interestingly enough, wisdom is personified as a woman in the Bible (Proverbs 4:8). Cherish and love her and she will add joy to your life. Abuse her, and you will not know true joy, thus missing out on the fullness of life that a proper appreciation of wisdom would have brought you. It is with the Bible as my guide I have avoided numerous pitfalls others fell into. It has kept me grounded and helped me chose not to pursue a life based solely on pleasure but purposeful progress.

Perhaps you are a freshman in college, with fresh memories of your sensational high school graduation, but remember to whom much is given much is required (Luke 12:48). Some of you may be experiencing a level of freedom that you previously did not have. Be careful because there is no such thing as absolute freedom. It is a lie, a thick illusion as deceptive as a mirage of a waterfall in the desert. Do not be deceived nor naïve–there is a price to pay for your actions. Neglect your studies or fail to use sound judgment and it will cost you. Trust me, you will be an adult far longer than a teenager or college student. Learn to think for yourself and cultivate this habit. It will save you from immense heartache and pain. Who knows, it may even save your very life.

* * *

Men must be ruled by God or governed by tyrants.

– William Penn

Only two things are infinite, the universe and human stupidity, and I'm not sure about the former.

– Albert Einstein

Our scientific power has outrun our spiritual power. We have guided missiles and misguided men.

– Martin Luther King Jr.

Chapter 1
Man's Desire for Guidance

"The *Dutchman* needs a captain." I pondered this phrase while watching the movie *Pirates of the Caribbean: Dead Man's Chest*. The character Bootstrap Bill uttered it after a heated battle with their foe Davy Jones, when his lifeless body lay vanquished on the deck of the *Flying Dutchman*. As his fellow crewmembers started to celebrate his defeat, Bootstrap Bill reminded them of the ill-fated bargain that was struck and had guided their fate. Anyone who is familiar with the sea is familiar with Davy Jones and his locker. He is a mythical, evil being who presides over everything disastrous at sea. Although in the movie Davy Jones was the captain of the *Flying Dutchman*, legend says it was the infamous Captain Van de Decken, who because of his arrogance, dared to defy nature, and he and his crew were cursed to sail the seas forever, never making port. Nevertheless, the words of Bootstrap Bill stuck with me, and I could not shake the thought that the Dutchman needs a captain.

Why do men so eagerly place themselves under the leadership of others? Why do we feel the need for a captain? It is obvious that someone always arises, assumes leadership by force, or is appointed by the masses. Nevertheless, history has shown time and time again the horror and cruelty of men who assume brutal leadership. This gives credence to the phrase, "Power tends to corrupt, but absolute power corrupts absolutely." Seemingly, with all of this knowledge at our disposal and the depravity of man being well documented, we still insist on playing the same old game, like an ill-fated chess player making the same bad moves over and over, yet expecting a different result. The outcome is assured. The only thing that is not is the name of the one who shall arise.

It reminds me of an incident in the Bible where the children of Israel tell their spiritual leader, Nathan, that they want a king (1 Samuel 8:4). Prior to this event Israel has no king. They are guided by the commandments of God, but their desire to have someone rule over them speak to something more perplexing. Scriptures declare that God has put eternity in our hearts (Ecclesiastes 3:11) symbolizing the desire in man for something he cannot explain. A greater call than one's self to aspire to a higher ideal of life would seem to have been placed there by God. Maybe as some sort of invisible road map in case we got lost, we would have something aid us on our journey throughout life. Whatever the reason, Israel wanted to be like other nations. They wanted a captain, a king, a man to glory in, someone tangible to heap their praise upon. After all, God is immaterial.

Where did this concept of a king come from in the first place? Could it be that man knows he is limited and feels in his heart of hearts his need for security? So instead of trusting in God, he seeks a counterfeit? We put flawed man over us in hopes of regaining the security we feel we have lost, in essence like Adam and Eve covering ourselves with fig leaves. Let's explore this concept of the counterfeit and flawed men replacing God. This very idea is doomed to failure because mortal men make pitiful gods. God is perfect, not able to be bought or sold, an omnipotent being who exists outside of time and space. Look at what you give up when you substitute man for God. You give up the infinite wisdom of a being who knows the very number of hairs on your hand, or as one older gentleman put it, "the number of hairs you once had." You give up a being of perfect love and tender heart. Contrast that with the deceitfulness of the human heart spoken of by Jesus. Scriptures declare that the heart of man is desperately wicked, so who can know it? (Jeremiah 17:9).

In my brief number of years on this earth, I have seen far too many leaders, dispensers of justice, and guardians of the truth, entrusted with the common good of society who have later been found to have committed gross injustices. Are these really the men we want over us, to judge us, plead our causes in the public square? They are fallible, not capable of dispensing what man truly longs for: perfect justice. Men are inadequate for the task of being God, too fallible and subject to their own desires. This impotence concerning our moral obligations knows no nationality or gender; all men and women are flawed. All too often when a bribe is offered to tilt the scale, it is taken. That is why the Bible says, "Put not your trust in man" (Psalms 146:3). He may have the best of intentions, but external and internal forces may drive him to abandon his principles.

Think of the difference with God at the helm instead of man, the peace and security that it garners. The Bible declares God who spoke the heavens into existence, formed man from the very dust of the ground with his own hands, who loves all of his creations equally (Genesis 2:7). He is impartial, cannot be bought, seduced, intoxicated, threatened, or bullied. He says in Isaiah 66:1, "I am God; heaven is my throne, and the earth is my footstool." He is omnipotent, omniscient, and omnipresent. The Bible also says that God is love (1 John 4:8). People all over the world consider love the highest virtue. Therefore, it can be safely assumed most men want to be loved. Because God is being pure love, you can rest in His presence. Even when God dispenses justice, you can count on Him to judge righteously (Genesis 18:25). That gives me comfort knowing I will get a fair hearing and equal opportunity for justice.

Let us look at the word as well the concept of

justice. *Webster's Dictionary* defines justice as the quality of being fair or just. Why do we feel that men should be fair or just? Where did this noble ideal of justice come from? In my humble opinion, without God there can be no true justice. If death ends all and there is no final reckoning, who is truly accountable for anything? I may pursue any action: rape, murder, theft, anything my sinister little mind can conceive, causing great harm and pain to people for no other reason than I wish it. Yes, society can impose its limitations and laws on me. However, I can break those laws, and when I am confronted about my actions, simply run in front of the police and die in a hail of bullets. If we hold to a naturalistic worldview, I am gone, so there is no ultimate accountability. Sure, there is a loss of life, but if there is nothing after death, big deal. We are all going to die anyway. Like the dinosaurs before us, we are just waiting for the next asteroid to hit causing our extinction.

This quandary of justice has only intensified my thinking on why I feel men seek out a master. Whether it is the captain of the JV team or President of the United States, the requirement is the same: lead us, for we are incapable of leading ourselves. What is it about the psyche of man that makes him feel like the proverbial sheep needing a shepherd? It reminds me when Jesus said, "I'm the good Shepherd. The good shepherd lays down his life for the sheep" (John 10:11). But scriptures also declare, "I praise you because I am fearfully and wonderfully made" (Psalm 139:14). I agree, when I look at the human body and think what a marvelous piece of engineering. If we are engineered to be marvelous, why then does Jesus refer to us as sheep?

In the eyes of God, we all became sheep when man decided to disobey God in the garden. We became vulnerable from the loss of strength that came from fellowship with God. Men have tried to fill the void with other things, but we deceive ourselves. We know we lost our way. We know the *Dutchman* needs a captain. Though the analogy I am using may be a fable, it fits with what we know of man and it has to suffice. I would like to revisit an earlier thought about the depravity of man and his propensity not only for good but also for great evil and destruction.

Man's propensity for self-destructive behavior does not fit the Theory of Evolution on two fronts. Let us look at the animal kingdom. It functions on a strict hierarchy, survival of the fittest and passing on your genes. A young lion sees nothing wrong with killing an old lion to pass on his own genes. That is the law of nature; no one will object to it. On the other hand, if a human did that, it would be considered cruel. It would seem that such limitations on our actions do not advance the species. Are we not wise enough to see that, or do we need a captain to point it out? Consider another example. Look at how a drug addict will shoot a substance into his veins for pure pleasure. Addicts may know it is killing them, destroying the body and mind; yet they persist. Their self-destructive actions do not lead to self-preservation or advancement of the species.

Let us return to the original quote by Bootstrap Bill, "The *Dutchman* needs a captain." We would like things not to be so, but that is the way it is. As with the ill-fated crew of the *Dutchman* so goes man in response to his ill–fated decision to replace God and be his own God. It would seem with all of our technological advancements, we could pull ourselves up by our proverbial bootstraps, freeing ourselves from our need for earthly captains, confidently summoning the strength and wisdom necessary to fix all the ills plaguing our societies. But the greatest minds collectively have not been able to do so. Keep in mind that what we see is not what God purposed for us. It also declares that man has a sinful nature, with evil in his heart. (Jeremiah 17:9)

The devil is given the distinction of being the ruler of this present world, the deceiver and the enemy of man, not God's enemy because God has no equal. This being was created by God. He is portrayed as once being good, so any power that this individual possess did not originate in him. As C.S. Lewis would put it, "Badness is only spoiled goodness." Satan influenced Adam and Eve to disobey God, therefore causing all of humanity to miss out on the life that God intended. The devil knowingly and willingly knew what he was causing. That speaks to his character. Any time you intentionally create a situation that causes people heartache and suffering, you are responsible for that pain.

The Bible declared that Satan convinced some of the angels to rebel against God. So we see there is an evil presence in the world that appears to be able to influence the hearts of men. It sounds farfetched, but it may explain why men can be so cruel to each other, sometimes for no other reason than the thrill of causing someone pain. There is strong evidence that Adolf Hitler and the Nazis were devil worshipers. Historians note after four years in Vienna, Hitler left and went to Munich. There he got involved with others who were dedicated to the pursuit of occult powers. It is a little known fact. The original members of the Nazis (National Socialist Party) were hardcore Satanists. It was the Nazis who led a willing Hitler into deeper levels of occult involvement. In fact, Dietrich Eckart, an occultist of the highest degree, and a practitioner of black magic, bragged before he died, "I have initiated him (Hitler) into the 'Secret Doctrine,' opened his centers in vision and given him the means of communication with the Powers...I shall have influenced history more than any other German." Hitler's occult activity could account for his almost supernatural ability to persuade decent human beings to commit unspeakable atrocities. Scriptures declare that the devil will someday be cast into the lake of fire (Revelations 20:10). We can ponder about his existence and think what we will. Is it not a fitting end for an individual who has enticed so many people to do evil?

This evil (if you want to use that word) supernatural or spiritual component should be considered a dangerous reality. It is amazing how devoted some people can be to religious leaders even when the so-called religious figure is obviously wrong. I recently heard about a situation where a so-called prophet was molesting young boys and girls, yet his followers still persisted in their support for him after he was incarcerated. I have nothing against organized religion, but I do have something against organized stupidity. Why do men follow so blindly? We can be so easily deceived, and as I stated earlier, religion can be a very dangerous thing, causing some followers to kill and turn their backs on their own family because a self-appointed spiritual guru deems himself to be God's messenger. It is also ironic that the one who was more than human, never sought to exalt himself? Jesus claimed to be God in the flesh (John 14:9), yet He did not go around showing off. The miracles He performed were for a specific purpose. Jesus was the meekest and lowliest of men, and he never sought to incite violence (Mathew 26:52). Jesus was a man of peace preaching forgiveness, tolerance, and brotherly love and did not want to be king even when the Jews sought to force it upon Him (John 6:15).

I am amazed that with all of our knowledge of what evil men have done in the name of religion, people still follow men like Jim Jones, who led 918 men and women to their death in the South American country of Guyana on November 18, 1978. David Koresh, whose standoff with the FBI, directly or indirectly caused seventy-two men and women and children to be burned alive. Warren Jeff still dictates the life and thoughts of so many individuals after being imprisoned. Joseph Stalin murdered millions of his own people; and finally, Adolph Hitler exterminated millions of Jews. The list goes on and on. I sometimes wonder why people would stay in situations that are so sick and twisted. Perhaps they have never known truth and only had lies fed to them their whole life. Even if someone were to take you out of these environments, the brainwashing can be so pervasive it would cause you to go back. Perhaps it would be too scary to live and think for yourself when you have had someone thinking for you for so long. There is also the added pressure of being told by some religious guru that to disobey them is to disobey God. It would take a miracle to break free and remain free.

So, yes, it appears that man is vulnerable in his need for guidance but has rejected his ultimate guidance from God, to whom ultimate power belongs. Scriptures declare," I make peace and create evil" (Isaiah 45:7). Not that God is evil, but He created the devil, who in turn chose to be evil. So in that regard, God created evil. God is the ultimate source of all power. He could have destroyed the devil long ago, but God knew He would not be just to punish the devil and the angels that rebelled against Him, yet overlook

Adam and Eve's disobedience. For instance, if you buy your teenager an expensive car and warn him not go to a certain part of town where they race for ownership of each other's cars and he comes home without the car, telling you he lost it on a bet racing, you could go take the car from the person he lost it to. But do you think that would be just, seeing how he lost it. In the words of character Dominick from the movie *Fast and Furious 8*, when his cousin told him he had lost his car racing, "A bet is a bet." But Dominick, not willing to see his cousin in distress, made an agreement with another party to get his cousin's car back. Dominick did in an epic race.

On a much grandeur scale, that is what God did. He paid the price for man's sins with His Son's life because He knew men how vulnerable men were without Him. God knew men would choose the wrong leaders. It is interesting when Pilate was seeking a way out of executing Jesus, he offered the Jews a choice: Jesus or Barabbas. They chose Barabbas. Pilate answered and said again unto them, "What will ye then that I shall do unto him whom ye call the King of the Jews?" And they cried out again," Crucify him." Then Pilate said unto them, "Why, what evil hath he done?" And they cried out the more exceedingly," Crucify him." And so Pilate, willing to content the people, released Barabbas unto them and delivered Jesus, when he had scourged him, to be crucified (Mark 15:17-23). The people's choice should not come as a surprise. All over the globe when men are faced with similar choices, the cry of the masses is the same, "Give us Barabbas."

* * *

There are no facts only interpretations

– Frederick Nietzsche

Rather than love, than money, than fame, give me truth.

–Henry David Thoreau

The truth is incontrovertible. Malice may attack it, ignorance may derive it, but in the end there it is.

–Winston Churchill

CHAPTER 2
IS THERE SUCH A THING AS ABSOLUTE TRUTH?

In the movie A Few Good Men, Colonel Nathan Jessup, played by Jack Nicholson, was under duress on the witness stand, and he blurted out the infamous phrase, "You can't handle the truth!" Similarly, Pontius Pilate somewhat ambivalent as to the conundrum the Jewish religious leaders had placed him in, facetiously asked Jesus, "What is truth?" (John 18:38). It seems that people all over the world want to know the truth. Webster's Dictionary defines truth as the property (as of a statement) of being in accord with fact or reality. According to our definition, facts should coincide with reality, not fantasy or personal opinion. Have you ever watched a court case or listened to an argument where there were not enough specifics or evidence to make a reasonable decision? Leaving you, perhaps like Pilate with the desire to know the truth. Why does it bother us so when we cannot get to the truth, or does it really matter?

Let us take it a step farther. Is there such a thing as absolute truth? Modern society wants us to say no, and we are drifting further way from the notion of absolute truth. So-called intellectuals have no problem with telling us there is no absolute truth. In their haste, they fail to notice that the statement, "There is no absolute truth," is contradictory. When a person makes it, all you have to do is say, "Is that the absolute truth?" The statement disqualifies itself because it is making a truth claim while denying there is such a thing as a truth claim. I must admit that something seems to be hidden in the argument against absolute truth. Like a free app that once you use it, suddenly all types of annoying pop-ups bombard your electrical device, and hidden charges are billed to you unawares. As long the argument against absolute truth is your default position, you can wiggle your way out of anything, lying if you need to because, after all, there is no absolute truth.

Keep in mind when you say something is true, you are also implying that the opposite is false. "Truth by its very nature is exclusive." Some might even ask, "How do you know something is true?" These individuals are holding to the idea of relativism—the concept that points of view have no truth or validity within themselves. But they only have relative subjective value according to the differences in perception and consideration. I would counter by saying, whatever happened to rational thought and observation? It bothers me that so many people are now being led to believe they can determine their own truth apart from fact and reality, even using what we now call, alternative facts.

If an incident is caught on video, apart from no credible evidence of tampering, is it not absolute truth? To deny this is to open up a whole other can of worms. Like the free app mentioned earlier, what is being smuggled in unawares? I believe it is a rearward assault against right and wrong. If you told most people there is no such thing as right and wrong, they would probably look at you rather oddly. But if you say there is no such thing as truth to some people, you sound sophisticated. You can disarm them in a subtle and seemingly intelligent fashion, freeing you to lie about an incident and secretly undermining the notion of right and wrong because all truth is relative. When you make a statement with an element of truth to it, is it actually true? If you ask a person selling you a car does it run well and he says yes, you would obviously be disappointed if it ran badly. When you ask the seller about it, he tells you that it runs well enough for him. So yes, the car runs, but it does not run well in the general sense. There is a measure of truth regarding the car, but you would still feel cheated.

Ask yourself what the world would be like if everyone made their own truth. Let us say you have a job interview scheduled for 1 PM. You arrive on time only to hear the interviewer say, "According to my watch it is 2 pm. You missed your appointment." Can you imagine the chaos? You probably could not have a functional society operating under the assumption that all truth is relative. Even when it comes to the study of religions, I follow the same philosophy I use in every other area of my life in regards to establishing truth. I follow the teachings of Jesus Christ, because I believe He was who He claimed to be, that He fulfilled the prophecies concerning the Messiah, which were written hundreds of years before His birth and that it corresponds with truth. You do not have to believe what I believe. You do not have to believe what I am saying. As a matter of fact, I do not want you to. That is why I give this challenge to you: take all the world's religions, strip them of their names and go strictly by the evidence. Then ask yourself: which one has the greatest likelihood of being true?

"Not knowing is no excuse for not knowing." A teacher told me that once after I had missed a test. I replied that I did not know because I was absent they day he announced it. I have seen instances where someone was an unwitting accomplice or naïve to the actions of a loved one. The question is, "Did he really not know or just chose to subconsciously not know?" An agnostic is a person who says he does not know if God exists, but I wonder is it a matter of evidence or is it a matter of not wanting to know. Not knowing seems like a safe position to hold. It is more acceptable to a broader section of society, certainly safer than choosing a side. Regarding religious truth, if you want to claim some aspects of the Christian faith but make no commitments to the claims of Jesus, there is a harsh reality you must acknowledge. Jesus Himself said, "For who so ever shall be ashamed of me and my words, of him shall the Son of Man be ashamed (Luke 9:26). So if Jesus was who He said He was, that is something you might want to think about. Yes, there is a risk in knowing. Can you handle the truth?

Truth is not always pleasant. Sometimes it shatters your illusions. Although the truth can be painful, it can also be freeing. It forces you to grow. I have learned not to shy away from the truth, but I must also tell you it takes resolve to handle it. Some people are unwilling to be honest with themselves, make the journey into their own soul. Hellen Keller said, "People don't like to think because when they think, they form conclusions and conclusions aren't always pleasant." Some conclusions, as well as some memories, are just too painful. The truth of the matter for someone may lie in acknowledging, "I was to blame, or I missed a valuable opportunity." Therefore, my present condition or what I am experiencing in life is a direct result of my poor judgment. Psychiatrists will tell you the worst thing you can do when something painful and traumatic happens to you in life is to try to pretend as if it never did. As I mentioned earlier, life can be very painful because the world we inhabit is not what God intended. It is not my intent to ignore how painful life can be. Some of the people whom you encounter in life will only want to use you for their own selfish gain, hoping you are naïve enough to let them. But Jesus invites us to rest in Him (Mathew 11:28) and in His words we find fullness of joy (1st John 1:4).

In regards to truth, excess information is not necessarily a good thing. With the advent of the Internet and twenty-four-hour news channels, there is no shortage of information and opinions. It is a far cry from when I was a child. I can actually remember when television would go off the air. Some of you may think that is funny, but I wonder what would happen if we shut off all the external influences just for a little while in order for us to meticulously process the overwhelming amount of information we are exposed to considering the fact anyone can say, write, or post anything at any time. They do not have to be qualified, their work does not have to be vetted, and they can just flood the airwaves with junk information, fake news, and everything else imaginable.

During my college years, I took a course in public speaking. I was not all that thrilled with the teacher. He was arrogant. But one thing he said stuck with me, which was, "Always use creditable sources and make sure you research your source materials thoroughly, in order to solidify your argument." That bit of advice has stuck with me through the years. For instance, I have no knowledge what so ever of what it takes to be a successful barber, yet I could write a book on how to cut hair. Someone could read my book, not knowing that I have absolutely no idea what I am talking about. However, since it is in print they will assume it must be trustworthy. The first thought I have when someone tells me something is, "How creditable and reliable is the information?" Repeating an event without fact checking it sufficiently can cause you great embarrassment. A listener or reader who knows what you are saying is not factually correct may challenge you on the validity of the truth claims you just made. Laziness in the area of proper fact checking and research can cause you to lose credibility and perhaps not be taken seriously in the future.

Social media can add a lot of information to any conversation, but I find it somewhat flawed. Do not get me wrong. I am not against technology or social media. But social media sites cannot adequately police their content. Some websites are even taking steps to combat fake news, which can be extremely misleading. I have seen countless videos on social media that are obviously wrong and falsifiable. The views being presented were not even close to being right. Yet, the Internet is free and accessible to everyone. It is up to you to understand that what is being presented may not necessarily be true? As Bill Gates stated, "Being flooded with information does not mean we have the right information." Having quality information is necessary for getting at the truth and making the best decision possible. It should be your endeavor to listen to all sides of an argument before you form your opinion. Double-check everything.

Truth is also your greatest defense to unrelenting disinformation. History is filled with men who knew how to twist the minds of their brothers and sisters to suit their agenda. Joseph Goebbels stated, "If you tell a lie big enough and keep repeating it, people will eventually come to believe it. The lie can be maintained only for such time as the State can shield the people from the political, economic and/or military consequences of the lie. It thus becomes vitally important for the State to use all of its powers to repress dissent, for the truth is the mortal enemy of the lie, and thus by extension, the truth is the greatest enemy of the State."

There is no such thing as a totally unbiased person. We are all biased in some form or another. But we should not let those biases get in the way of truth, which sort of leaves me somewhat puzzled concerning critics of religion. I do not care what some so-called religious fanatic does in the world. Prominent atheist and critics of religion somehow manage to overlook the obvious atrocities of some religions and direct all their rage and disgust of religions towards Christianity. I am still trying to figure out that correlation. I am not saying Christianity should not be criticized. If the criticism is valid, I see no problem with it. But let us be intellectually honest in our critique of the influences of all religions on society.

Jesus set himself up for some heavy criticism by saying, "I am the way, the truth, and the life. No one comes to the Father except through me" (John 14:6). Those are some pretty heavy words for an insignificant carpenter. Oddly enough, Jesus said He would be killed and rise again on the third day. (Mathew 16:21.) His claim is so astounding, that after His death the Roman government placed soldiers outside His tomb to guard His body. Believe what you will about Jesus. Feel free to criticize every aspect of the Christian faith, but what we do know historically is that the tomb of Jesus was empty. His body somehow mysteriously vanished while being guarded by what would have to be considered Rome's elite Special Forces. A testament to truth of the empty tomb is that His body has never been produced. Many theories have been advanced to deny the resurrection of Jesus Christ, such as the disciples stole His body while the Roman guards slept, or Jesus was not really dead, or the women went to the wrong tomb. But such theories have long been discredited.

One noted author Frank Morris wrote a book entitled, *Who Moved the Stone*, in which he examined the historical evidence for Jesus and His resurrection. He stated that he purposely chose to focus on the last seven days of the life of Jesus because it was clear of any supernatural elements. Morris's examination of the evidence of the life of Jesus led him to believe that the evidence for the crucifixion of Christ and His bodily resurrection was credible. I can imagine the title of his book gives us a glimpse into his thinking concerning how a body could disappear under such intense observation. I find it hard to believe someone could roll a stone weighing one to two tons away from the tomb without awakening the Roman guards. But as we established earlier, truth should coincide with fact and reality. If it does not, it is not truth; it is just wishful thinking.

* * *

It's very unlikely that a universe would exist uncaused, but rather more likely that God would exist uncaused.

– Richard Swinburne

The deep emotional conviction of the presence of a superior reasoning power, which is revealed in the incomprehensible universe, forms my idea of a God.

– Albert Einstein

I have explained the phenomena of the heavens and sea by the force of gravity, but I have not yet assigned a cause to gravity.

– Isaac Newton

Chapter 3
God Does Exist

The existence of an omnipotent eternal being who created all that we see is sure to stir up passionate debate among people. Some would probably argue as to the very idea of the existence of God being worthy of serious debate, instead encouraging people to shed their belief in such fairy tales. But is God truly a fairy tale or a coping mechanism created by primitive man? When we say God, some may ask what God we are talking about: the God whom Einstein revealed as the superior reasoning power behind the universe or the Aristotelian God possessing immutability, immateriality, omnipotence, omniscience, oneness or indivisibility, perfect goodness and necessary existence. I am not seeking to validate all such religious beliefs, so it will be my endeavor to express my belief in the existence of the God of the Bible, who shares similar characteristics with the Aristotelian God, that is, who is eternal, without beginning or end, who spoke the world into existence and sustains it by his power alone (Colossians 1:10). All other religious worldviews must defend themselves, hopefully in a reasonable manner.

I will not be so arrogant as to say anyone can prove beyond a shadow of doubt that God does exist. But I will focus on arguments that provide a strong case for His existence, endeavoring to keep my argument for the existence of God as simple as possible, arguing from an Ontological stand point—stressing the existence of God and his being: Cosmological, or dealing with the origin and general structure of the universe; Teleological, which is based on the perceived design in the natural and physical world; and from the moral perspective, which examines how humans from all cultures seem to have a sense of right and wrong or moral normative.

Let us start with the ontological perspective. Why do so many people believe in beings greater than themselves? Where did this confident belief come from? Since the dawn of time itself, men have held a belief in deities, and it has persisted throughout the ages. It is so entrenched into the psyche of man that one has to wonder why. Is belief in God truly a coping mechanism to explain what primitive man did not understand, a God of the gaps theory, meaning I cannot explain it, therefore, God must have done it. I think it is much deeper than that, to pin the beliefs of millions of people–past, present and future–on mere superstition, seems to be rather disingenuous. Surely, many of these people are entitled to the legitimacy of being competent. Just because a person lived thousands of years ago does not mean he was less intelligent than you and I. In the interest of fairness, it should only mean he did not have access to the information we possess today.

I think that point is worthy of further discussion. I would hate to be judged by someone in the future, as being unintelligent because I did not have access to the informational gadgets that only exist in their time period. In my humble opinion, just because a person was riding in a horse-drawn carriage and I the latest model automobile, it does not mean that they were any less competent or incapable of rational and intelligent thought. Surely God could communicate with them on their level as He does with you and me.

Some skeptics even suggest no sane person could believe in God. But prior to Charles Darwin and his Theory of Evolution, creationism was the prevailing understanding of most people. It was a common belief that man was created by God, and even Darwin himself was once a theist. Darwin even stated, "[Reason tells me of the] extreme difficulty or rather impossibility of conceiving this immense and wonderful universe, including man with his capacity of looking far backwards and far into futurity, as the result of blind chance or necessity. When thus reflecting, I feel compelled to look to a First Cause having an intelligent mind in some degree analogous to that of man: I deserve to be called a Theist."

Isaac Newton, the Father of Modern Science, saw no contradiction in believing in science and God. People still considered themselves to be intelligent while maintaining their belief in a Creator. The two major thoughts of the origin of man to this very day are evolution and creationism. Why should a person be ostracized when he has researched the evidence for the reliability and authenticity of the Bible and that evidence has led him to believe in a creator?

Critiques have also suggested that God does not have a physical body; therefore, He could not exist. But God does not have to be seen in order to bAs a being He can be known by His actions or an agent that causes things to happen. In that regard, God is a real being like you or me. Just because you have never laid eyes on someone physically does not mean they do not exist. If your wife comes in with her hair done, you do not have to see the hairdresser to know he or she exists. You see the results. When we look at the universe and its apparent design, we see that which symbolizes a highly advanced intelligence. You do not have to see God; you see the outcome of his actions in the obvious design of man and the universe.

Let us address the cosmological aspect. When the evidence that the universe had a beginning and was not eternal was first presented, it was resisted. Not because of the evidence, per se, but because some felt it would give too much confidence to those who believed in the Bible. The Bible clearly states, "In the beginning God created the heavens and the Earth" (Genesis 1:1), proclaiming that the universe was not eternal as some had believed. Physicist Edmund Whittaker even stated, "There is no ground for supposing that matter and energy existed before and were suddenly galvanized into action. It is simpler to postulate creation "ex nihilo" divine will constituting nature from nothingness."

It would seem that some people would accept any theory for the beginning of the universe as long as it is not God. No matter how fanciful that theory maybe in its own right, even coming up with desperate or unsatisfying ideas such as the multiverse theory, proposing there are multiple universes and life just happened to have arisen in ours, thus making it possible and more likely to have arisen somewhere else in an alternate universe. This theory ultimately goes nowhere because no one attempts to explain what is responsible for putting out the various differing universes, like a cosmic printer spitting out multiple copies, which leads us right back to square one. Who designed the printer? Richard Swinburne stated, "It's crazy to postulate a trillion (causally unconnected) universes to explain the features of one when postulating one entity (God) will do the job." I agree, and in my view it fits with the Occam's razor principle, "Pluralitas non est ponenda sine necessitate. Or the simplest answer is the best answer.

Richard Dawkins even went so far as to say that God is too complex to an argument on the question of the universe, but Richard Plantinga pointed out that by Dawkins' own definition, God is simple and not complex because God is a spirit, not a material object and hence does not have any moving parts. I would also disagree with Mr. Dawkins because if you go by the evidence that the universe had a beginning and it appears to be intelligently designed, that premise alone is all you really need to formulate your worldview. So the assertion that God is too complex or His beginning is really irrelevant. Who could comprehend a being of God's immense power? God has always been God. He is eternal, uncaused. Prior to the accidental discovery of evidence for the universe having a beginning, scientists were fine with the assumption that the universe was eternal. They had no knowledge of how it came into being; it just existed from eternity past. So why cannot we apply that same rationale to the existence of God. He is eternal without beginning nor end, father nor mother.

This dilemma not only exists in getting a first cause to the beginning of the universe, but also with the beginning of life–how you get life from non–life. The world-class scientist and Nobel Prize winner Francis Crick stated "An honest man, armed with all the knowledge available to us now, could only state that in some sense, the origin of life appears at the moment to be almost a miracle, so many are the conditions which would have had to have been satisfied to get it going." Paul Davies stated, "The problem of how meaningful or semantic information can emerge spontaneously from a collection of mindless molecules subject to blind and purposeless forces presents a deep conceptual challenge."

Let us now examine the teleological aspect,

which deals with the obvious design aspects of the universe. Removing God as the causal agent for the existence of the universe leads to an argument not from design but to design. It also sets the universe on an unguided path with no forethought or planning involved. Random matter that came out of nowhere just happened to have arrived at order and given rise to complex sentient beings capable of asking, "Who created me, and why am I here? Such a thought seems ridiculous. Nature even obeys laws and no one can explain how these laws came to be. Whenever you have a law, however small it may be, there must be intelligence behind it to give an explanation for why it is needed in the first place.

It seems logical to think that if the universe has certain obvious design features, there must be a designer. When you look at the location of the Earth and all the various conditions necessary for life as we know it, it is a stretch to imagine it is all by chance. As theoretical physicist Freeman Dyson stated, "As we look out into the Universe and identify the many accidents of physics and astronomy that have worked together to our benefit, it almost seems as if the Universe must in some sense have known that we were coming." So the conditions that gave rise to life as we know it were prearranged. In my opinion to get all the laws and factors that govern our universe by chance is like placing a weight on the accelerator of a car, putting it in drive, and expecting it to drive safely across the United States. There is no scientific evidence that nature behaves in such a way. Again, inanimate matter just does not arrange itself in nature. I have never seen the leaves in my yard organize themselves into neat little piles in order for me to put them into trash bags.

Even males and females seemed to be designed to complement one another. I have often wondered how nature unguided just happened upon the male and female design for reproduction. It seems rather odd that random nature, with billions of years and all the various methods of reproduction could have come up with a simpler more efficient method. I have even heard people postulate the first human was a female who reproduced asexually. Why would nature create a being that would go through the trouble of developing a womb in order to give birth to a male being? He, in return, would then mate with a female counterpart in order to produce more offspring. It just seems absurd the more you think about it. Our design fits more with the account in Genesis when God made male and female (Genesis 5:2).

Lastly, there is the moral argument. Why do we view some things as obviously wrong? One has to wonder how an amoral universe can produce conscious sentient beings with this strong sense of morality. As German philosopher Immanuel Kant stated, "Two things awe me the most: the starry sky above me and the moral law within me." This innate sense that some things are obviously right and wrong exist in all societies. It may produce varying laws of conduct, but it is, however, there. People expect some form of moral normative, where they can tell someone, "You ought not to have done that?" When a person is seated and gets up to retrieve something and someone hops in their seat, all onlookers would probably consider that wrong, and say, "You should know better." But why do we assume they should know better?

This innate sense of a moral law has led some to question why there is so much evil and suffering in the world. However, there is a flaw in their reasoning. If you say you do not believe in God because there is too much suffering in the world, you would have to ask yourself, how do you distinguish between good and evil? To quote Ravi Zacharias again, "When you say there's such a thing as evil, aren't you assuming there's such a thing as good? And if you're making the distinction between good and evil, you're depositing a moral law to distinguish between good and evil. If there's a moral law to distinguish between good and evil, then there's a moral lawgiver. And if there is no moral lawgiver, there's no good and evil. And if there's no good and evil, what happens to the question?" So we see that the question of suffering is only valid if God, or, at least, some moral lawgiver exists.

Why do we feel so strongly that this world is a mess? C.S. Lewis stated, "How would you know something is crooked if you didn't have anything to compare it to? So, if were a product of time and chance, we should have no reason to believe that the world is anything other than what it should be. At the very least, we should not be able to claim some basis for comparison of messy versus clean, bad versus good." Could these feelings and possible hatred of God somehow validate His existence? It would seem obvious that you cannot hate someone or something that does not exist. Some people even hate God because they feel He let them down. I must admit, I have been there a time or two when I thought God let me down. If there is no God to begin with, why do we have this strong sense of betrayal? When I watch certain debates and see such anger and passion coming from people arguing against the existence of God, I cannot help but wonder. What happened to you that caused you to hate God so much? That level of passion does not come from nowhere. There is something beneath the surface you are not telling. You do not get mad at someone who supposedly does not exist.

I recently heard an atheist say, "Why doesn't God intervene more in the lives of men? Why doesn't he heal a paralyzed veteran in a wheelchair or a person who has lost a limb? He is certainly capable or does he not care? He obviously does not realize that God has already acted in human history with the sacrifice of His son and giving us His word. God performed all types of miracles for the children of Israel, and many of them still did not change their behavior. They just kept waiting on the next miracle. And certainly, if a person is determined not to believe, he will not. As David Hume proudly asserted, "Miracles do not happen." Why would not God heal a paralyzed individual, or an individual who has lost a limb? It is a fair question, and it seems logical. However, the more I thought about it, the more I began to change my mind. Is God supposed to heal everyone who asks him regardless of if they believe in him or not or even healing a person enabling them to do greater evil? I believe too much intervention by God into this temporal realm could be problematic. To have a stable world would necessitate miracles be few. God knows how to strike the right balance when it comes to interjecting Himself into suffering humanity. So on the surface, having God intervene miraculously into our everyday lives seems wonderful, but it would not change the hearts of men.

* * *

You can speak of the science of ethics but you can't speak of the ethics of science.

– Albert Einstein

Equipped with the five senses, man explores the universe around him and calls the adventure science.

– Edwin Hubble

Now I am become death, the destroyer of worlds.

– J. Robert Oppenheimer (quoting the Bhagavad Gita)

CHAPTER 4
THE VALUE AND LIMITATIONS OF SCIENCE

"It's alive!" cried Dr. Frankenstein as his unholy creation lumbered off the exam table. It is with this phrase that I would like to comment on the value and limitations of science. How ironic that the author theorized Dr. Frankenstein could produce life from the decaying body parts of various corpses. Another conundrum would be the various mixtures of DNA as well as blood types. A tale such as this could only exist in one's imagination, a doctor raiding the graveyards at night for suitable materials. The guardian of health, moonlighting as a grave robber. The eerie sounds in the darkness disturbed by his tools sneaking in and out of the earth, uncovering what was once laid to rest. The story declares with his human effort, Dr. Frankenstein finally pieced together something destined to be less than human. As Doctor Frankenstein hoisted his lifeless creation towards the night sky through an opening in his laboratory's roof, lightning flashed, the thunder roared. Nature was in agreement that something unnatural was in the making. Finally, lightning struck the lifeless corpse, an unintentional gift from the heavens, and with this energy coursing through his creature's veins, a glimpse of life appeared. As Dr. Frankenstein peered at his creation, one would have to wonder, was it sheer brilliance or stupidity? Like the famous adage, it is not wise to mess with Mother Nature.

I do not by any means want to belittle the scientific achievements of men. Science has added and will continue to add much-needed value to our lives. I also think it is naïve to believe that science will ultimately answer all questions concerning life. Some have even suggested that what science cannot teach us, we cannot know. Such a statement dismisses all other forms of knowledge and can be easily debunked by the parameters of naturalism because the statement itself is not scientific: it is philosophical. I personally believe science will ultimately give us the means to inflict more suffering on our fellow sisters and brothers. Such a statement may be highly offensive to some. A testament to its validity is this: With all of man's potential, what is his most destructive scientific achievement? It is debatable, but I think it has to be the nuclear bomb.

When the first atomic bomb exploded over Hiroshima, more than eighty thousand souls vanished in one second, incinerated into nothingness, leaving behind a ghostly dark outline on the surface. Not to say scientific advancements are desperately needed. We need advancements in medicine and all the areas of life, but science is not an entity: it is a process. Exposing another limitation of science, its inability to create ethical barriers. Albert Einstein stated, "You can speak of the science of ethics but you cannot speak of the ethics of science." Science cannot be treated as an entity because it is devoid of a conscience. Science gives men the means to create the atom bomb but does not tell them if they should use it.

There are some things science cannot account for. Chemists can mix a certain chemicals for a perfume, but cannot tell you if your wife will like it without performing tests on her. Which I am sure most women would not find romantic. Scientific testing can tell me the genetic makeup of a child, whether he or she has fast twitch muscles or good hand/eye coordination, but it cannot tell me if the child will even like sports, or work at all. He might be a deadbeat. Yes, science can measure the weight of a heart, but it cannot measure desire. There is no test for that. It is like a scene in one of my favorite movies, *Gattaca*. It takes place in the future where babies are engineered to their parents liking and society's elite standard. In the movie, Vincent was conceived the old- fashioned way, proving to be a liability in a world of genetically engineered people. Vincent pays someone to introduce him to Jerome, who is genetically engineered, but is crippled from an accident. The process is illegal but Vincent hopes by assuming Jerome's identity he can get into Gattaca, an elite aeronautics institution. Vincent having met his benefactor, Jerome, personally, discovers Jerome has been engineered with everything he needs to get into Gattaca except the will to do so. The movie prompts you think about the limitations of genetic manipulation and the power of the human spirit.

Debate is brewing over an emerging technology called (CRISPER) Clustered Regularity Intersected Short Palindromic Repeats. It functions by slicing DNA to remove bad code and replacing it with good code. As you can imagine, its emergence has raised a lot of concerns over the potential to modify DNA. Questions have been raised regarding the elimination of certain diseases as well as the ability to engineer human beings. One noted pioneer of the technology is biochemist Jennifer Doudna, who some think will eventually win a Nobel Peace Prize for her work in the field. She touts the promising future of CRISPER but freely admitted as the technology advanced, important conversations will be necessary to deem what is acceptable as well as off limits. The advancements we are making in the field of science, including genetic manipulation and cloning, have to be navigated cautiously. Who knows what man will conceive, given his propensity for violence and war. This aspect of man's psyche has to be accounted for. How long do you think it will be before we start genetically modifying human beings not only for service but war?

The escalation will probably follow this path: Country A genetically engineers its soldiers to gain an advantage on the battlefield over country B. Then country B decides to engineer its soldiers to be bigger, stronger, and faster than those of country A. Country C, not willing to be outdone, decides to engineer its soldiers to outdo countries A and B. Science may help rid the world of certain diseases and health problems, greatly improving our quality of life, but to think that science will solve the problem of man's inhumanity to man is unrealistic. I am afraid our desire to dominate other men will only produce bigger, stronger, faster, smarter killers. I think my point is sound, and I only dealt with the first three letters of the alphabet. What do you think is going to happen when the rest get involved?

I would also like to reiterate my point about the nuclear bomb. Nothing on earth rivals its power and destructive ability. This was evident from its inception. Robert Oppenheimer who was among the scientists responsible for creating the first atom bomb, when faced with the realization that the weapon was going to be used, quoted from the Bhagavad-Gita "I am become, death the destroyer of worlds." The world still bears the scars of the bombs impact today at Hiroshima and Nagasaki. The bomb produced vast devastation and untold suffering, all of it from the mind of man. Yes, the human mind is awesome. Many scientists still do not understand what the mind is its true potential, given what we have accomplished with it so far. I believe man's mental capacities have been limited by God himself because of our sinful nature, for this the world should be grateful.

Why did we not end world hunger, or poverty, or even design products for the masses to advance human dignity. Instead, with all of our brilliance and potential, we built the nuclear bomb, something to possibly end life on Earth, as we know it. The possibility will always be there as long as we have nuclear weapons. President John F. Kennedy found that out when he was being pressured by his advisors to invade Cuba during the Cuban missile crisis in October 1962, as well as to bomb Russia. Thank God President Kennedy did not listen to his advisors, because unbeknownst to the American government, Fidel Castro had already told Nikita Khrushchev, the Russian president, if any American troops tried to invade Cuba, to set off a nuclear bomb. The invading forces would have been incinerated, and it might have been the end of civilization, as we know it. Amazing that instead of using our minds to produce life, we chose to find a way to produce more death.

Sam Harris says he is concerned about religious extremists getting their hands on nuclear weapons. He should focus his attention on why man felt the need to create something so destructive in the first place. His bias when it comes to religion is evident. You do not have to be religious to be a homicidal maniac. Hitler was not religious, but can you imagine him with nuclear weapons? North Korea is an atheist regime, yet the world shudders at the thought of them having nuclear weapons. Religious extremist do pose a threat to society, but so does any idiot with charisma, propensity for violence, or desire for world domination.

As I pen these thoughts, a photo has captured the heart of the world, the photo of a dead three-year-old boy whose lifeless body washed ashore on the beach in Bodrum, a Turkish resort town. His family was fleeing the war-torn country of Syria. The boat they were on sank in the rough seas; the father survived, but his two sons drowned. The image of that little child lying face down on the beach said what words could not. His lifeless body lay there so peaceful and serene; he did not appear to be dead but only asleep. His little body was then carried by an unidentified person in uniform; truly the person who said a picture could be worth a thousand words is right. The father apparently did what he thought he must in order to survive. It is a sad reality of the horrors that can accompany life.

Science can tell us the universe had a beginning, but it cannot tell us why there is a universe in the first place. It can only quantify what it sees. The observable universe can be measured but where did the power come from to set it in motion? No one knows. One writer stated, "Science can tell you how the heavens go, but can't tell you how to go to heaven." Sam Harris said, "Religious faith is on the wrong side of an escalating war of ideals, science must destroy religion". That statement, on its own, is very disturbing. Let us contrast that with a statement by the Catholic Church, "There can never be a contradiction between faith and science because both originate in God. It is God himself who gives both the light of reason and of faith". It would seem that religion does not want to destroy science. Even with the abuses in Christianity and the Catholic Church, many believers and I myself maintain a high regard for science. In my opinion religion can never destroy science because if you do, you destroy God. The laws that govern our universe are fixed. I believe that God set them in motion. These laws seem to be constant; anyone seeking to deny these laws simply is not wise.

Science cannot answer why is there something instead of nothing? When does nothing decide to become something? The same question can be asked regarding the origin of life. When did chemicals in a pool of stagnant water become animate and then sentient beings? How did these chemicals decide to become conscious? How does consciousness come into being? Better yet, what is consciousness? That is a tremendous point of contention right there. It is a stretch to believe these chemicals had the awareness to upgrade itself. Even our computers do not upgrade themselves; programmers do. A computer that automatically updates itself is definitely not thinking; it is simply following a program from a higher intelligence. How did pond scum write its own genetic code? All our genetic code is information, albeit complex information. Charles Darwin's theory of evolution never touches on the subject of creation. His work is centered on adaptation and evolution. Darwin starts with Pre-existing matter and what he observes. How the single cell organism come into existence is not adequately addressed by his theory. He only used his knowledge to observe life. He never proposes the theory for the origin of life only the origin of the species.

As stated earlier what makes up the human mind? Scientists still do not know much about it. I recently read an article about how some scientists theorize that storage capacity of the human brain is virtually endless. Therefore, it is possible to live eternally with your mind. Think about it. Scientists can map the human brain without truly understanding or knowing how it works. I can recall dates, memories, images, faces and all sorts of cool stuff. If you cut a human brain open, you will not see a memory or anything, just wrinkled tissue. Not to mention consciousness, we still do not know how it arose either. Your ability to think proves you are a conscious being, but how it came to be no one really knows. As Roy Abraham Varghese stated, "We are conscious, and conscious that we are conscious. No one can deny this without self-contradiction—although some persist in doing so." This also fits with the creation narrative that God formed man from the dust of the earth and breathed into his nostrils the breath of life and man became a living soul (Genesis 2:7). What happens to people when they die? Do they cease to exist or does the spirit live on? Anyone who has ever looked at a dead body will tell you it is just an empty shell. Something is missing. I believe it is the breath of life that comes from God. When your time on Earth is finished, it goes back to God.

Some people say that the biblical account of creation is simply absurd. I admit there are some things in the Bible I do not understand. When God made man, he was made with the appearance of age. So it is no stretch of the imagination to think that God could have made the Earth with appearance of age too. God being an eternal being he is not bound by time with the Lord a day is like a thousand years and a thousand years are like a day (2 Peter 3:8). So when you say God made man on the six day, it may not mean a twenty-four hour period. Being a license practical nurse I have had a fair amount of study in biology and of the human body, leading me to believe that it is an engineering marvel. The cell rivals any super computer in complexity; it is a proverbial storehouse of information. And then consider your muscles, the very fibers- how they contract and when they are over exerted; they begin to build up lactic acid prompting you to rest. You perspire in order to cool off. When you are cut, protective measures kick in to stop the bleeding by clotting.

Scientists define certain biological functions as being operationally impossible. It simply means that there is no way it could happen. It is highly unlikely that ribosome's advanced knowledge of how to assemble proteins evolved. Some scientists theorize that the chance of one protein molecule forming by chance is operationally impossible. So if we look at all the various proteins that make up the human body, it would stand to reason, that something so complex and functional could not be the product of a mindless unguided process. With this knowledge at my disposal, although I love science, I have to believe that the origin of man is beyond the realm of science.

Evolution has not proved to be an adequate explanation for the origin of man, where there is insufficient evidence. It asks you to take a leap of faith. Asserting that nature over the course of billions of years by trial and error and natural selection could produce all that the various forms of life we see today. One would have to wonder. "What prompted inanimate nature to work towards an unknown end goal?" I think the unlimited time explanation for the origin of man has some merit. But without the luxury of observing evolution over the course of billions of years, we have to use our rational observation. Take the automobile for instance; we know when and why it was invented. You can see how it has changed from its inception until now. Not only can we see the changes in the automobile, we know what is guiding these changes. Evolution simply does not answer these questions.

My skepticism concerning Darwin's theory of evolution was echoed by Darwin himself. He thought in time science would validate his theory. Darwin even stated, "To suppose that the eye, with all its inimitable contrivances for adjusting the focus to different distances, for admitting different amounts of light, and for the correction of spherical and chromatic aberration, could have been formed by natural selection, seems, I freely confess, absurd in the highest possible degree." So if man did evolve from primates over the course of billions of years, should not the fossil evidence be abundant? Fossilized embryos have been found in the Cambrian layer of the Earth. If embryos can be preserved over the course of millions of years, certainly the evidence for the supposedly transitional missing link skeletons should be abundant. We see they simply are not there and science has failed to explain their absence. Science then, at the very least, is not without its limitations.

* * *

If atheism solved all human woe, then the Soviet Union would have been an empire of joy and dancing bunnies instead of a land of corpses.

– Jones C. Wright

The universe we observe has precisely the properties we should expect if there's, at bottom, no design, no purpose, no evil, no good, nothing but blind pitiless indifference.

– Richard Dawkins

To the dumb question, 'Why me?' the cosmos barely bothers to return the reply, 'Why not?'

– Christopher Hitchens

Chapter 5
What Atheism Really Offers

It is hard to believe at one point in the history of our nation, being on the verge of death was considered fashionable and attractive. During the 1900's an estimated 100,000 Americans died each year from what was then known as consumption (so named because of the consuming effects it had on the body). Today we refer to it as tuberculosis, or TB. During the early twentieth century it was one of the leading causes of death. It claimed the lives of the old, young, rich, poor, or famous. In a twisted kind of way, people somehow found the sickening deterioration of the human body and subsequent death as beautiful, similar to the heroin chic fashion trend of the early 1990's, when models were depicted as anorexic and sickly, mimicking the destructive effects of heroin on the body of addicts. The atheist Richard Dawkins stated, "What I can't understand is why you can't see the extraordinary beauty of the idea that life started from nothing–that is staggering, eloquent, *beautiful thing*, why would you clutter it up with something as messy as God?" It is with this thought in mind that I look at what atheism truly offers, a beautiful death.

Once you take away God, no matter how eloquent you make your argument for His absence or proclaim how freeing it will be, the final outcome is death. As a theist and someone who believes in a loving Creator, I believe that when I die I am going to be with that Creator—not fading into a bitter oblivion of nothingness. Considerable thought and research has gone into my examination of how life offers its meaning. The atheist's worldview rests on the premise that there is no God and removes any sort of afterlife beyond death from the equation. This life is all you have, and death ends all. Recent atheists have gone to great lengths to portray the suffering, cruelty of this world and subsequent death as beautiful, encouraging people to shed their silly beliefs in a Creator. I hold to biblical worldview, so my defense of God will be limited to the God of the Bible, in other words, the God of Judeo-Christian beliefs and heritage which offer me eternal life, encouraging me to see violent deterioration of the human body as unnatural and proposes it was never God's will for man to die.

Going by the account provided in Genesis, God created two human beings called Adam and Eve and placed them in the Garden of Eden. There was no such thing as death, only eternity with Him (Romans 5:12). God commanded them not to eat of the Tree of the Knowledge of Good and Evil, telling them," "The day you eat of it you shall surely die" (Genesis 2:17). Death is a result of them disobeying God's commands by listening to the being the Bible refers to as the devil (Genesis 3:1). Now, you may say, "Wait a minute. They did not die." That is correct, at least partially, as they did eventually die. The death God was speaking of was spiritual. For the wages of sin is death; but the gift of God is eternal life through Jesus Christ our Lord (Romans 6:23). This spiritual death leads to the physical. The scriptures declare that Jesus told a young man to follow him. But he said, "Lord, suffer me first to go and bury my father." Jesus said unto him," Let the dead bury their dead"

(9:59-60). The young man's relatives were of course alive but did not have spiritual life, which comes through Jesus Christ.

Some may challenge the legitimacy of my belief system and life after death. Atheists must realize that there's a belief system too. Its proponents gather all the evidence and form their own conclusions. Some atheists have made it their top priority to get rid of religion because they feel it is not rational. In spite of the overwhelming evidence that religion can play a positive role in the lives of people, I do not know why some atheists are so irritated by religion. It seems to me that if atheism has such an obvious advantage over seemingly irrational believers, it should be pounding religion into the ground, and with the aid of science, utterly wiped it out centuries ago. There is certainly enough ammunition to blow God out of the water, but it has not. People, it seems, are willing to ask the deeper questions about the existence of God, suffering and the meaning of life. Many who believe in God can acknowledge abuses and issues in religion and know that such things are man's fault, not God's.

As a Christian, I try to look at the evidence for God's existence, evidence such as the historical existence of Jesus, the empty tomb and His bodily resurrection, and the reliability of the scriptures. Although I feel the evidence for Christ's claims of divinity is sound, ultimately it involves some form of faith, and that position is always vulnerable to attack. Some atheists may perceive this vulnerability as definitely falsifiable, but they fail to realize their position also involves a measure of faith. Atheists only believe in that which can be proven, but that leaves room for beliefs they themselves hold that cannot be disproven. As such, there is hypocrisy.

Atheists also talk about decisions being made with bad evidence. The late atheist Christopher Hitchens stated, "That which can be asserted without evidence can be dismissed without evidence." I would counter with a question: who decides what constitutes good and bad evidence? What constitutes good for one may not be for another. One noted astronomer Frederick Hoyle thought it was impossible for life to have arisen on Earth strictly by chance. He supported the Pan

Spermia Theory, proposing aliens from another planet seeded the earth, thus producing life. Hoyle supported the theory because the impossibility of life arising on Earth by itself seemed to be good evidence in favor of that theory. Many others thought his theory was invalid because that impossibility was not good enough evidence to support the existence of the aliens themselves.

One world-renowned atheist, Anthony Flew, wrote numerous books arguing there is no God. After much thought and research, he had a change of mind and wrote a book entitled "There Is a God" denouncing his atheism. He stated, "The only satisfactory explanation for the origin of such "end directed, self-replicating" life as we see on the Earth is an infinite, intelligent mind." Flew stressed how DNA influenced his change of mind, stating, "What I think the DNA material has done is that it has shown, by the almost unbelievable complexity of the arrangements which are needed to produce (life), that intelligence must have been involved in getting these extraordinary diverse elements to work together. It is the enormous subtlety of the ways they work together. The meeting of these two parts at the right time by chance is simply minute. It is all a matter of enormous complexity by which the results were achieved, which looked to me like the work of intelligence." Flew stated his change of course was consistent with his long established philosophical principle of following the argument no matter where it leads. To quote an unknown detective from the crime show Forty Eight Hours, "I love evidence; it never lies. It can be misinterpreted, but it never lies." I agree evidence should trump personal prejudice.

Flew and many others have also said the problem of evil and suffering led them to believe there was no God. But I find a certain incoherence with atheists concerning the concept of evil and suffering. The problem with their argument is how do you know when something is evil? A naturalistic worldview postulates that man arose from matter, which arose from nothing in an unguided random process. From that starting point, I do not see how you get a rationale for morality? Some have suggested that our sense of morality evolved over millions of years as a result of men seeking to better get along with each other. I would challenge that by saying, if the concept of morality as we know it evolved, can it not also devolve? I mean if we accept the premise that life arose from nothing, we should expect nothing from life. I am not saying atheists cannot be moral or good. I have had many interesting conversations with nice atheist co-workers, but there is no point of reference for their moral beliefs. As GK Chesterton stated, "Morality like art consists in drawing the line somewhere." So in their critique of believers, they have left themselves open to argument in defending their moral position. If the theist has to defend his moral conviction, the atheist must also. Supposing that if life without God would be better, where is the evidence?

Atheists are very vocal about instances of violence committed by people of faith but quickly dismiss the abuses committed by regimes headed by Stalin, Hitler, Mao Zedong and Pol Pot. Rationalizing they were not really atheist regimes, they attempt to sidestep this issue with the grace of a hippo ballerina. Some atheists say Christians are atheists towards Zeus, Thor, and other gods. The argument continues that the real atheists just take a step further, also eliminating Yahweh, the God of the Bible. That argument, to me is misleading. It smugly assumes that Christian faith is not supported by credible evidence, such as the transformed lives of Jesus followers, or the existence of the church—and can therefore be dismissed as easily as the myths of old. Jesus was an actual historical person, but Zeus was not. Although past generations might have believed in such false gods, the truth would still be the truth even though clouded by superstition and lack of adequate information. I do not see anywhere in recorded history where hundreds of people could not lift Thor's hammer. If there was creditable evidence for such an event, it should be considered. It is, however recorded that Jesus was crucified and his tomb was empty and hundreds claimed to have seen Him after His resurrection.

I have confessed that I am not a Bible scholar. I am, however, a common man who has read numerous books on religion and philosophy and listened to countless debates by so-called experts. I am also attempting to use reasonable observation and judgment, so be the judge yourself if what I say makes any sense at all. On what grounds do we base our assertions that anything is wrong? Notions of right or wrong cannot come by just time and chance with no guidance. Christopher Hitchens once stated, "Rape was not wrong. It simply was not good for society." I thought that is absurd, but maybe it is just an anomaly, until I heard Sam Harris make a similar claim that rape has gotten us this far but is no longer advantageous. This is a gigantic problem for atheists regarding certain behaviors that may require a moral judgment. It forces them to explain on what grounds they base their morality.

When it comes to atheism as a means of comfort, it amazes me to see people applaud some of the points atheists make at certain debates. After the applause, I often think, "The only thing he offered was death in the form of comfortable ideas." I am not saying people should not take comfort in their beliefs, but just because something is comforting does not make it true. Jesus testified of an afterlife that will be filled with unspeakable joy in the presence of an all-loving

God for those who trust in him (John 14:2). Like many others, I have tried to get justice and accountability without God, but the issue remains unresolved. If there is no accountability for anything, then life is the crudest thing ever imagined. Think about it. Someone born into a rich family can live their life in opulence and luxury with no regard for anyone or anything. They can be suffering from "affluenza", which means they are somehow too rich and privileged to know right from wrong. Another person can be born into abject poverty, be abused mentally, physically, sexually in the most hideous ways. In regards to suffering, Richard Dawkins has stated, "In a world such as ours, that's just how it is: too bad." That is just your lot in life. Time and chance say you have to suffer, while another enjoys his temporal life.

It is not respectful to call people stupid or illogical for believing in God, when billions of people hold to a belief in God in some form or another. I am not seeking to legitimize all such religious beliefs. I am merely stressing the existence of a large number of beings who believe in the supernatural. I even find certain logic in Pascal's *Wager*, which seeks to justify Christian faith, is by considering the various possible consequences of belief and disbelief in the God of Christianity:

> If we believe in the Christian God and that He exists, the argument runs, then we will receive a great reward in heaven. Conversely, if He does not exist, then we have lost little or nothing. If we do not believe in the Christian God and He exists, the argument continues. If He exists, then we will receive an infinitely great punishment in hell. With the reverse corollary following that if He does not then we will have gained little or nothing. The possible outcomes of belief in the Christian God, then, are on balance better than the possible outcomes of disbelief in the Christian God. It is better to either receive an infinitely great reward in heaven or lose little or nothing then it is to either receive an infinitely great punishment in hell or gain little or nothing.

Richard Dawkins recently stated, "God is dead—have fun." The famous atheist Fredrick Nietzsche popularized this phrase "God is dead". Who are we kidding? If God is dead, there are some serious implications here. As Aristotle stated, "Nature abhors a vacuum." Someone or something has to take Gods place. I shudder to think what the world would be like in the absence of a transcendent, omniscient, omnipotent, all loving being in which our morality has been anchored. One noted apologist Ravi Zacharias stated, "It would leave man with a desire for pleasure or power." I agree. At least Nietzsche was honest enough to realize the deep philosophical implications of getting rid of the omnipotent God.

I feel the new atheists do not seem prepared to deal with consequences of a God-free universe. They want the morals of society without the moral law-giver from whence morality originated. Even Dawkins, when pressed on the reality of living with a Darwinian world view, stated, "No decent person wants to live in a society that works according to Darwinian laws ... A Darwinian society would be a fascist state." Hence the argument that the atheists' beliefs are often connected with fascist regimes like Hitler's. I agree with Dr. Dawkins that the logical outworking of the Darwinian world-view would be fascism. The strong dominate the weak.

That is the law of the jungle: only the strong survive.

Where is the comfort in a God-free universe? How does it alleviate suffering? When a person loses a loved one, there is no comfort-just death. In the atheist's worldview there is no rhyme or reason for anything. That is just life. So what if your love one died? Be thankful for the time you had with them. Oh, you have a diagnosis of cancer? As Christopher Hitchens would say, "The party's still going, but you have to leave." He considered this world a party. For some people in this world life is not a party, but a nightmare. In my opinion getting rid of God creates more problems. When you get rid of God, you also get rid of moral imperatives such as not stealing, not murdering, and so on. One wonders who the pawn in this game of life really is.

One trick the Devil often implores is the "God is trying to keep you dumb argument'. This trick is similar to a conversation I observed between Professor John Lennox and a questioner. The question posed by the individual was, "Why would you serve a God who wants to keep you dumb?"

Professor Lennox cautiously replied, "That is an interesting question, but I cannot help recall it was first raised by the snake." As you can imagine, such a response generated quite a bit of laughter. When God placed Adam and Eve in the Garden of Eden, everything was permissible--except for one thing. There was only one law: not to eat of the Tree of the Knowledge of Good and Evil. I believe if God thought it was necessary, He would have eventually exposed Adam and Eve to the nature of evil its horrors. Adam and Eve were made innocent and did not need to know the reality of sin. God, like a loving parent, gave them parameters for their lives, and our world bears the scars of man disobeying God. So where then is our hope? In my opinion to leave man without God is to leave him in a psychotic state. I think this psychosis is evident by man finding the decay of the beautiful human body as attractive.

I say that to reiterate my point that Satan offered Adam and Eve something they did not need. But before we concede the point that God is trying to keep man dumb, I truly believe there are some things man should not know. When the

Almighty God gave them the command not to do something, it should have been respected and followed by Adam and Eve because God is loving and only had their well being in mind. God never intended them to know evil because they were not equipped to defeat it anyway. So to say that God was trying to keep them dumb is an unfair criticism. The same offer of freedom from God's commands, the right to be your own God and define right and wrong for yourself that was offered to them, is also offered to you and me. After all, why would a loving God object to you knowing good and evil? In essence, you do not need God; you can be God. The devil knew full well what his intensions were to make God the enemy. With this subtle argument, Adam disobeyed God, plunging the world into the chaotic state we see today.

It is not reasonable for me to get rid of God because finding a suitable replacement would be impossible. Fredrick Nietzsche in "The Parable the Mad Man" voiced similar concerns in getting rid of God, proclaiming, "Is not the greatness of this deed too great for us?" Some have even suggested we should replace God with ourselves. I find that thought utterly ridiculous. What power do we as mortal men truly possess? William Shakespeare wrote, "All the world's a stage and we are merely players." If that is indeed so, without God, death triumphantly takes center stage, and we must exit stage left as insignificant actors to be seen no more. If death permits, you may be allowed a final curtain call in appreciation for your performance in life. But without God there is nothing beyond the grave and no foundation on which to base the higher ideals of life such as love, integrity, morality, or valor. I believe there is plenty of evidence for the existence of God on which to base them. But to base them on the premise of atheism with no ultimate accountability for anything because death ends all, seems to me, an inadequate foundation to base anything substantive on.

* * *

If God does not exist everything is permissible.

– Fyodor Dostoyevsky

Whenever I hear anyone arguing for slavery, I feel a strong impulse to see it tried on him personally.

– Abraham Lincoln

There is no king who has not had a slave among his ancestors, and no slave who has not had a king among his.

– Hellen Keller

CHAPTER 6
WHAT'S WRONG WITH SLAVERY?

I know slavery is a big issue and a painful and traumatic topic for mankind. As well it should be. The thought of a human owning another human being seems immoral and unnatural. Slavery has also been used as a centerpiece in the argument against the character of God or the existence of a God at all. Once a coworker stated, "Slavery was one of the main reasons that lead me to believe there was no God." He is certainly not alone; many do not believe a loving God can allow such cruelty. In my humble opinion, slavery is only wrong if God exists because it would take the existence of a Creator to speak to the validity of individual worth. If there is no Creator, we are at the mercy of pure Darwinism, which stresses adaptation or survival of the fittest doctrine proposed by Herbert Spencer. There are no rules, but only brute strength. Take what you will if you are big and bad enough to get away with it.

America as a whole has had a truly traumatic experience with slavery, which has after- effects to this very day. This period in history has led to much criticism of some Americans. Slavery was not started or invented in the United States. It has existed since the dawn of man in every corner of the globe. People have long been enslaving others; because it receives greater condemnation in the United States does not absolve other nations of their injustices concerning slavery. One person deprived of their freedom is still one too many. Even in the famous Dred Scott case, where the judge ruled Mr. Scott was merely property.

Using the Bible as a framework concerning the issue of slavery, we see that God was clearly specific when He created man. The Bible states "Let them have dominion over the fish of the sea, and over the foul of the air, over the cattle, and over every creeping thing that creepeth upon the Earth" (Genesis 1:26). God never said anything about men having dominion other men in the way most contemporaries understand slavery. God had establishes his order; man simply to obeys. It is the fall of man that leads to the violence and oppression we see today. Some have used the instances of violence in the Old Testament to try and support slavery or to build the case against God of the Bible. Some critics say, "Aha, God condones slavery." Yet they fail to acknowledge this current world system is not what God intended.

We must also consider whatever God or spiritual force you claim to serve must also be held accountable for allowing slavery to exist in our world. As the philosopher Epicurus stated, "Either God wants to abolish evil and cannot: or he can, but does not want to; or he cannot and does not want to. If he wants to but cannot, he is impotent. If he can and does not want to, he is wicked. But, if God both can and wants to abolish evil, then how comes evil in the world?" Epicurus presents a fair assessment of God, in light of the pain and suffering that exists on our world. We cannot exclusively condemn the God of the bible for allowing slavery and yet allow all other forms of spirituality a free pass. I have often heard people say, "Why God did not give a command condemning slavery?" If he did, it still does not mean men would obey it. The commandment, "Thou shalt not kill" has not stopped people from committing murder.

I am not seeking to justify slavery but giving a voice to why I feel God gave laws concerning it. I think the following passage sheds some light on the subject. When scribes and Pharisees came to Jesus asking him, "Is it lawful for a man to divorce his wife for just any reason?" (Mathew 19:3). Jesus went on to reiterate the sacredness and seriousness of marriage. The scribes and Pharisees then responded, "Why then did Moses command to give her a certificate of divorce and put her away?" Here is the accusation. "If it is wrong, why did God give laws permitting it?" Jesus said unto them, "Moses because of the hardness of your hearts suffered you to put away your wives: but in the beginning, it was not so" (Mathew 19:8). God's original intent for marriage was for Adam and Eve to be in a monogamous lifelong relationship, but man strayed. Just as divorce was not his will, neither was slavery. So I submit that God never approved of slavery. He allowed it because he knew how evil men could be to each other.

Women at that time in society were vulnerable to all sorts of abuse and injustice. So God gave Moses those commands to try and ensure women had some form of protection and maintained their dignity as human beings. God only gives laws concerning slavery in an attempt to maintain some form of human dignity in a world where not only the hearts of men were hard towards each other, but mainly God. In the beginning, it was not so.

Man's inhumanity to man is well documented. God never approved of or condoned slavery. He allowed it because man in his fallen condition was capable of tremendous cruelty. Noted atheist Sam Harris pulls a sleight of hand when it comes to the cruelty of man. He states, "We have been slow to recognize the degree to which religious faith perpetuates man's inhumanity to man." Such a statement falsely assumes that religion leads men to unnecessary violence. But what accounts for the atrocities committed by people who do not believe in God? God's view on human equality is evident from the start. He never gives man dominion over other men. God only ordains government when men assume the right to rule over each other.

We must also keep biblical slavery in its proper context. Their form of slavery was totally different from ours. It is more along the lines of an indentured servant. If men could not support themselves or their family, they can offer themselves and their children for service. Keep in mind this current world system is not God's will. The laws he gave regarding slavery were not meant as directives, but as guiding parameters. He is dealing with fallen men who, because of Adams sin, now were responsible for being their own gods. They failed; the scriptures declare, "God saw that the wickedness of man was great in the Earth, and that every imagination in the thought of His heart was on evil continually" (Genesis 6:5). And so God set the law to govern His people in the treatment of their fellow human beings. Israel is not the only nation with laws regarding slavery; such laws exist throughout the world.

Not all forms of oppression are as obvious as physical slavery. Men have been finding convenient ways to abuse others since the dawn of time. Some religions put you in an inferior role simply by birth. Many Hindus believe men are not created equal. Once you are born into a lower class you cannot advance beyond it. Their reasoning is if you were bad in a previous life, you deserve to be treated like an inferior creature. It is a misconception that the Bible is the only religious book with laws concerning slavery. I have confessed that I find it interesting when various groups are discussing the negative influences of religion on society. The Christian faith seems to be public enemy number one. We must also consider the fact that apart from God, man can produce no logical reason why slavery is morally wrong, operating from a purely naturalistic worldview that nature has no morality.

Charles Darwin knew this, and it was the one thing that frightened him about his theory. Darwin stated, "Nature was bred in tooth and claw." The strong dominate the weak, like the young lion that kills the older lion. Once he has killed his rival, he then kills his offspring, spurring the lionesses to go into heat. He does all this in order to reproduce and pass on his genes. It was upon this merciless, naturalistic worldview that Hitler proposed his final solution in dealing with the Jewish people, stating, "I do not look upon the Jews as animals. They are further removed from animals than we are...Therefore, it is not a crime to exterminate them, since they do not belong to humanity at all." Frederick Niche went so far as to say that, "Equality was a lie perpetrated by inferior people." Niche would be right if we were holding to a naturalistic worldview. We must accept its consequences. I am sure we have all seen firsthand how the strong prey on the weak, and the only way not to be prey is to be stronger or smarter than your enemy. As a former prison guard, I know firsthand that statement is true.

The violence in the Old Testament is disturbing. How do we reconcile these two opposing views: one of God being a God of love and the other where God ordered the killing of thousands of people? God ordering the death of the Amalekites on the surface may seem cruel, but God often uses human forces to administer His discipline. In Genesis 15:13, 16, God says to Abraham, "Your descendants will be strangers in a land that is not theirs, where they will be enslaved and oppressed four hundred years.... Then in the fourth generation they shall return here, for the iniquity of the Amorites is not yet complete." God's ways are past our understanding. But if you look at it, all souls belong to Him (Ezekiel 18:4). He has the power of death and life. When God takes a life, He has the ability to restore, even more than what was lost. The Scriptures declare that before God went to destroy Sodom and Gomorrah, He talked with Abraham. God told Abraham what He was about to do. After reasoning with God, Abraham asked Him a critical question: Shall not the judge of all the earth do right? (Genesis 18:25)

The calling to do right by our fellow brethren has always been present in the Christian faith. It was the Christians that challenge the system of slavery not only in America but also throughout the world. If it had not been for Christians calling their brothers and sisters to a higher standard, who knows what the world would look like today? William Wilberforce and many others dedicated their lives to the eradication of slavery in Britain. William Wilberforce was encouraged by John Newton, who was a slave trader turned preacher. John Newton is also credited with writing the hymn "Amazing Grace," but critiques of Christianity are surprisingly quiet on this point.

Critics of the Christian faith also overlook the violent death of Jesus on the cross, while accusing God of promoting cruelty and slavery, but say nothing about the manner of Jesus' death and how He was tortured by men and never cursed them. The Scriptures declare that Jesus was God in the flesh (John 1:1), so a big question is, "What was God doing on the cross? Why did God subject himself to such cruelty at the hands of beings He created? That point alone makes you think, if God was as mean and cruel as some people say, He definitely would not have subjected Himself to the humiliation of death on a cross.

While we are on the subject of violence and cruelty, I will also like to add a note about abortion. Abortion is legal in America and many places throughout the world. You can abort a baby for any reason. Those reasons can be as minor as not wanting to lose your figure, not being ready for a baby, or as serious as not wanting the child because of rape. I find it worth mentioning that ever since abortion was legalized in 1973 because of Roe v. Wade, millions of babies have been aborted. I have seen estimates at 53 million in America alone. If finite man with limited knowledge and no ability to create life compared to God, how can we claim the moral high ground? At least God has the ability to resurrect life; man has zero power to do so. Therefore, it would seem logical that if the omnipotent God ordered the extermination of thousands to fit His purpose. How can we as a modern society condemn God when we have aborted millions in America? Not to mention the tens of millions of abortions in other nations because it suited our purpose. You can say what you will, but I believe that is a very valid point worthy of serious thought and reflection.

If we are going to criticize God for instances of violence in the Old Testament, we must also keep them in their proper context. At the time of those commands, society was primitive. There were no police forces, no 911 to call in case of emergency, no jails or prisons, or anything resembling the modern forms of society we have today. I think we have to be intellectually fair and honest, consider stoning, which seems barbaric to us today. But let us remember iron was not readily available, not everybody had axes or swords, and they certainly did not have guns. One of the big questions in a primitive society was how do you promote justice? Put yourself in their shoes. You have this violent criminal with no remorse. Do you let him go free because there are no prisons or do you take his life for everyone's safety? You would not have had modern weapons. If stoning is an option, then so be it. Stoning also was a community event because the judgment was supposed to be fair and unanimous. The whole community was involved, signifying we are all in agreement and we all share the responsibility for the action. Societies must have law and order to survive; without it, you would have complete pandemonium.

Even if you think my point is cruel, I offer this scenario. You are in your home, and an individual breaks in to kill you and abuse your family. You cannot call 911, nor do you have no gun or knife. What do you do? He has made his intentions clear. You do not have a weapon, but you have a large rock. Do you beat him to death with the stone or let him kill you and your family? I would beat him to death with the stone. I may not like it, but I would do it. So with that thought in mind, how could I truly criticize God for allowing the murderer or rapist to be stoned? I would also like to present this scenario. If there was a global catastrophe or apocalypse and man had to start all over at square one. "What laws could you enact to govern a primitive society?" I have a feeling that the laws and Old Testament would be sufficient for governing such a society.

I am not at all advocating mindless violence, but we must be honest, not only in our critique of God but of man also. We see firsthand how evil man can be to each other, so this idea that man does not need a proverbial dictator in the sky to control his actions is misleading and insufficient. Why do we need laws in the first place? History has shown us that men are good at passing laws and equally as good at breaking them. I know a case where an individual was treated with a slap on the wrist for driving drunk and killing several people. The lawyer somehow convinced the judge that his client was suffering from affluenza and was too rich and privileged to know right from wrong, consequently he was sent to a fancy detention center.

I mentioned earlier the judge declared Dredd Scott to be mere property. How does a rational person arrive at that conclusion? I submit the judge did know the consequences of his actions, for ideals and ideologies have consequences. Holding to an idea or worldview and trying to live it out in whatever way you can, there would be a price to pay. If your ideals are good, your reward in life will be good; however, if they are bad, you may advertently or inadvertently cause significant pain and suffering.

Slavery existed in other places in the world, but I feel it took a nefarious turn in America. When people convinced themselves that their fellow human beings were not even human. Such thinking is not only dangerous for the victim, but it is equally destructive for the abuser. In order to deprive a person of their humanity, you must first give up yours. You cannot maintain your humanity if you are seeking to deprive another human being of his or hers. In order to convince a man he is not human, you are going to have to commit inhumane acts on him. No sane human being can commit inhumane acts on another without incurring tremendous psychological damage. That is why men deem other men to be inferior or not human. It frees them of their guilt of the savagery they have inflicted against their fellow man.

It is a common practice among men who want to abuse another person or ethnic group. The abusers must first rationalize in some way or another that the victim somehow is inferior to them, thus mistreatment is acceptable. The abusers can conveniently clear their conscience by avoiding the psychological damage that comes from such inhuman behavior or even believing the person deserved the abuse. The same was with slavery in America and anywhere else men committed such atrocities.

In America our moral foundation is based upon Judeo-Christian belief. It inspired these words: "For we hold these truths to be self-evident that all men are created equal and endowed by their Creator with certain inalienable rights." Inalienable rights can neither be given nor taken away. If they cannot be given or taken away, what are their origins? They are bestowed upon us by our Creator.   At present America is being pressured to rip up its moral foundation. Even when Americans strayed from its moral obligations of liberty and justice for all by allowing slavery and the unjust treatment of their fellow Americans, the consequence are still there staring them in the face. The higher ideals of love, justice, and moral responsibility to our fellow man requires this great foundation of individual worth bestowed upon everyone by God. If your ideals are small, and you do not consider all human life of much significance above other animals, it does not matter what you base them on.

Men do not really need the Bible to justify slavery. Distorting some cherry-picked verses is a convenient means to help alleviate their sense of depravity. Search your own heart. Have you ever rationalized that you are better than someone else? They deserved to be treated as you saw fit. The abused must be seen as being inhuman because the moment the abused becomes human, the abuser ceases to be seen as human.   Also if instances of violence have led you to believe there is no God, you have a bigger problem. If God is a human construct, we cannot blame the institution of slavery or senseless violence on Him because said construct (God) does not exist. So, it would stand to reason that slavery is solely a man-made institution.

I have heard prominent atheists call slavery evil, but what does the word "evil" really mean. Is evil not intangible? Some people go to such extremes as to say there is no such thing as evil. Knowing when you declare some action to be evil, you must then define and defend the reasoning that led you to your conclusion because the only laws that the universe follows are the laws of nature, and nature does not tell men how to treat one another. There must be a higher law that supersedes the laws of men. During the Nuremberg trial, the Nazis proclaimed they were only following the laws of their country and had done nothing wrong concerning the Jews. Robert Jackson, chief counsel for the United States during that time, argued that there was a "law above the law" that stood in judgment on the arbitrary opinions of men. Apart from a divine Creator bestowing worth of all men equally, the Nazis would have been right. There is nothing wrong with the stronger animals eliminating the weaker ones with man being the most dangerous animal of them all.

* * *

"Science without religion is lame, religion without science is blind."

–Albert Einstein

If the rate of expansion one second after the Big Bang had been smaller by even one point in hundred thousand million million, it would have read collapsed before it reached its present size.

– Stephen Hawkins

Our galaxy, the Milky Way, is one of 50 or 100 billion other galaxies in the universe.

– Neil DeGrasse Tyson

CHAPTER 7
THE GRANDEUR OF THE UNIVERSE

"The key is under the mat." This familiar statement would be mundane if it was not for who owned the key. In a scene in *All-Star Superman*, when Lois Lane asked Superman if his key was safe under the doormat, he replied, "Yes," and encouraged her to pick it up. She could not. He went on to tell Lois that he carved it from dwarf star material. A teaspoon of matter from the heart of a dwarf star can weigh 15 tons, Superman could leave his key under the mat because it weighed tons; carved out of a substance so immense and dense, it was such as no ordinary human being would ever stand a chance of lifting it. Let us not get overly scientific about the gravitational pull of an object that heavy or why it did not crack the surface on which it lay. My purpose is simply to deal with the magnificence of the cosmos.

We cannot really understand how immense and grand the universe is. Scientists date our universe to be around 13.7 billion years old and Hubble estimates that there are about 50 billion galaxies in our observable universe. If each galaxy contains (on average) 50 billion stars, then the observable universe could contain 5,000,000,000,000,000,000,000 stars. That is beyond belief. What is even more amazing is that the universe is still expanding. If you were traveling at the speed of light, 186,000 miles per second, you could not cross the universe because it is expanding faster than the speed of light. One should wonder why the universe is still expanding. I believe when God said, "Let there be light," (Genesis 1:3) it sprang forth, and has been going ever since. The Scriptures declare Gods Word shall not return unto him void (Isaiah 55:11). God's Word being infinite and all-powerful, the universe had no choice but to keep going because God never told light to stop.

When I think about the vastness of the universe, billions of galaxies and billions of planets, the universe potentially allows everyone to have their own planet. As a believer in God through Jesus Christ, the Bible tells me one day I will be in the presence of this omnipotent being who created it all. I will be an eternal being, not bound by time and space. Without those limitations you could explore all the wonders of the universe, perhaps even watch a star go supernova. The Scriptures declare, "Eye has not seen, nor ear heard, neither has it interred to the hearts of men what God has prepared for those that love him" (1 Corinthians 2:9). Look at the limits we are placing on ourselves when we say our temporal existence on planet Earth is all there is to life. So much of the universe would be good for nothing; I mean nobody is using it. When I say "we", I mean mankind.

Limiting ourselves to man's view of our place in the universe, thus removing God from the paradigm would be as absurd as the Queen of England living in Buckingham palace, yet only staying in the bathrooms—even if the smallest bathroom in the palace may be larger than some penthouses in New York City. When you give up on God, eternity, and the supernatural, you are in essence living in the bathroom. The Scriptures say that the heavens declare the work of God (Psalm

19:1). The universe is a self-revealing revelation. We are all awe struck at times by an event, a moment, perhaps a sunset. Not even a Rembrandt or Picasso painting could stir the echoes of the soul, like the sun sneaking away to its place of rest—such a moment needs no words. Could Beethoven, Bach or whoever you fancy compare to the sound of wind blowing through the trees, or the sound of raindrops dancing ever so gently on a tin roof?

Man can only theorize about the origin of the universe and life. Scientific advancements have allowed us to explore the universe in greater detail but have not revealed anything of certainty about its origin. Scientists do not know what to do with this quandary. How you get a first cause to the beginning of the universe? It is an established fact based upon the accidental discovery by Arnold Penzias and Robert Wilson in 1962, when a hum in their equipment that was later explained as remnants of background radiation left over from the beginning of the universe. Their discovery will later be termed "the big bang theory". We have to be careful with the term "big bang". It can be somewhat misleading. I prefer the term "singularity" because when you think of a big bang, perhaps you are like me and probably think of an explosion. In order to have an explosion, you must have physical matter, time, and space. Prior to the singularity, these things did not exist.

The idea of a singularity as the astronomer Joseph Silk observed, is "completely unacceptable as a physical description of the universe...an infinitely dense universe is where the laws of physics, and even time and space, breakdown." This is where I feel the world renowned Professor Stephen Hawkins made a monumental blunder so obvious a layman like myself noticed it. When he stated, "Because there is a law of gravity the universe can and will create itself." Wait a minute, if the universe did not exist, that means gravity did not exist because it is a byproduct of the universe. It presupposes the existence of something to explain its own origin. It is like me saying my mother exists because of me.

The Kalam Cosmological argument in a nutshell states everything with a beginning has a cause. It has been given new life when Professor

William Lane Craig proposed it this way. First, everything that begins to exist has a cause of its existence. Second, the universe began to exist. Third, therefore, the universe has a cause to its existence. Fourth, since no scientific explanation (in terms of physical laws) can provide a casual account of the origin of the universe, the cause must be personal (explanation is given in terms of a personal agent). I do not care how scientists try to get something out of nothing, nothing will always be nothing. At no time can nothing be something. If I give your girlfriend a box with no ring and she opens it and finds nothing, she would probably look at you rather oddly and say, "There is nothing in here." Do you think she would be fine if you told her, "Baby, it is ok because nothing is really something'?" She would certainly walk away bewildered, and I do not think she will be walking down the aisle to marry such a nut case. Nothing is only something when desperate scientist wants it to be.

I must add the Bible told of the greatest event in the history of mankind, long before it was established scientific fact. The Scriptures declared in the beginning God created the heavens and the earth (Genesis 1:1). When the theory of the universe having a beginning was first proposed, it was resisted because some believed it would give too much confidence to those who believe in the Bible. Now, I ask you, is this scientific rationale or merely a personal bias? Richard Dawkins even stated, "You cannot go by common sense when it comes to the beginning of the universe, where something came from nothing." It would seem it is perfectly fine to suspend common sense when it comes to the beginning of the universe from a scientific standpoint. Or to say that the universe just is, it is not okay to do so when you believe that a creator was behind it. The Nobel laureate Arnold Penzias stated "The best data we have concerning the big bang, are exactly what I would have predicted had I nothing to go on but the five books of Moses, the Psalms, the Bible as a whole."

One of the limitations of reality is the very concept of time itself. What is time anyway? As we noted time and space had beginning. I am reminded of a drawing I saw that depicted the beginning of the universe springing forth in one direction, like a cone shape. I cannot help but think that if the model is accurate, the point of origin by simple definition must be eternaWe are all limited by time and somehow it seems unfair. Why do we feel this way? The universe compared to man seems to be eternal; a billion years here or there is still a billion years. Have you ever gotten lost in the moment when hours seemed like minutes? I remember one particular night; I was working on an art project. My brother said goodbye and walked out the door. It seemed like a short time later he walked back in. I asked, "Back already?" to which he replied, "What do you mean? I've been gone four hours." I was so wrapped up in what I was doing hours seemed like minutes. To live without time means a thousand years can feel like a day to piggyback on an earlier thought. Would it not be amazing if you were standing beside God, watching a star being formed and you asked Him, "How long have we been here?" And He replied," About a thousand years?" That would be awesome with God there is no concept of time—just eternity.

We must also take into consideration the

marvel our planet is. It is in the Goldilocks zone for human existence neither too hot nor too cold. Our planet has water that nourishes life. Scientists consider water to be one of the major indicators of a planet's ability to support life. How is it that our planet just happens to be in this zone? What are the odds? As scientist scour the universe, they are finding out how unique this planet is? Earth has the right orbit around the sun, allowing us to have seasons. We have the right size moon to regulate our oceans. The prevailing thought from the beginning was that as technology advanced we would find numerous planets like ours capable of supporting life, but the opposite has occurred. Truly, the chances of finding another planet like ours seem astronomical. It would appear for the moment that we are truly alone. We have sent messages through various means into the cosmos, yet we have not gotten a response. This can mean there are highly advanced being watching us, or we are highly advanced beings watching the heavens, with our place in the universe seemingly unique.

The laws of our universe are precise and follow certain very fine-tuned guidelines. All the elements and forces work together, forming synergy. We must ask ourselves why are there set laws that govern our universe, such as Newton's first law of motion. An object at rest remains at rest unless acted upon by an external and unbalanced force; an object in motion remains in motion unless acted upon by an external unbalanced force. The laws of thermodynamics explore any of the three principles governing the relationship between different forms of energy. Have you ever heard someone say about a piano, an exotic sports car, or expensive piece of machinery? This is finely tuned, that means it is operating to a manufacturer's preordained specifications, allowing it to run at its most optimal and efficient level. Anywhere you have fine-tuning there is a mind behind it.

Another issue is the order from chaos theory or the Law of Entropy. We never see things move from chaos to order; normally it is the other way around, moving from order to disorder. Take a look at The Great Pyramids of Giza with their immense size and brilliant engineering. What happens when people are no longer there to maintain them? Nature tends to slowly reclaim the elements take from her, tearing down the carefully cut blocks of stones. As this process continues pyramids will sink slowly sink back into the earth or take, for example, a piece of steel. It will eventually rust and disintegrate, going back to the elements from whence it came. This notion of a random explosion causing raw energy and unknown elements to arrange themselves with pinpoint precision seems to defy logic. Like water running up stream, it simply does not happen.

Let us explore the rationality of the universe. Why does the universe make sense and why do we expect it to? Nature obeys natural laws, or a regularity or symmetry in nature. We have an ability to use laws of nature predict the movements of the heavens? We can calculate the Earth's gravitational pull and the amount of thrust required to break free of it. Enabling us to safely land on an object in space and return to Earth. As stated previously there are fixed laws governing our universe, there are no particular reasons why these laws are in existence in the first place. Albert Einstein sated, "The harmony of natural law reveals an Intelligence of such superiority that, compared with it, all the systematic thinking and acting of human beings is an insignificant act." Einstein theorized you couldn't go faster than the speed of light. Why is that? I disagree with Einstein not on physical plain but metaphysical. I believe there is something faster than the speed of light. The speed of thought. When the disciples were in room the room the bibles says Jesus appeared in the mist of them. Jesus passed through a solid structure.

Let us not lose our sense of wonder at the vastness and magnificence of the universe. It would seem we try to ignore the beauty of the heavens but cannot fully. Why do we gaze into the stars? Camping is a multimillion-dollar industry. Why do we spend so much to be out under the heavens on starry nights? As the total eclipse on August 21, 2017 neared. The excitement and anticipation the eclipse prompted people to travel from all over the globe to witness it. Some even said it was the event of a lifetime. It would seem that man let down his guard to pay homage to the grander of the universe, perhaps reigniting something in the soul we cannot fully explain. As one news reporter said, "The overwhelming power of the eclipse made us look to the heavens once more, taking our focus off the things going on around us." As I personally observed day interrupted by night, thinking this is such a powerful event. After attempting to witness the eclipse through sunglasses that offered insignificant protection, I was not foolish enough to risk damage to my eyes by looking at the eclipse without the proper eyewear. So I graciously bowed to the overwhelming power of the universe and its creator.

Going back to the beginning of this chapter, Superman's key was safe because it could not be lifted by an ordinary human being, but I believe we as believer in Christ have something greater. After all, Superman's key could only unlock the door to the fortress of solitude. Believers in Christ have a key that unlocks the very universe itself, and the many mysteries that plagued us. Although the universe is cold and dark, like moments in our lives can be, Jesus lets us know we are not alone. Knowing that sometimes pain can be a universe in and of itself. Our key also unlocks the human heart, allowing love (which is after all the supreme force) to flow through men. This key can be lifted by anyone. I have heard people say death is not the end but a door into a greater existence. Not only is Christ the key, but He is the door also (John 10:9). On our own, we cannot unlock the mysteries of the universe, but Jesus has unlocked them for us. Jesus, the word made flesh, is the creator of all things. All physical matter was spoken into existence by God. The only thing that God personally put His hands on was man, when He formed him from the dust of the Earth (Genesis 2:7). Science can only measure the observable universe, but Jesus observed the universe when it sprang into existence.

* * *

All religions are exclusive.

– Ravi Zacharias

Christianity is a very historical religion-it makes claims that are open to testing.

– Lee Strobel

After I set out to refute Christianity intellectually and couldn't, I came to the conclusion the bible was true and Jesus Christ was Gods Son.

– Josh McDowell

CHAPTER 8
CHRISTIANS ARE SO NARROW MINDED

I was having a conversation with a co-worker in which I expressed my belief in Jesus. Almost immediately she responded, "You Christians are so narrow minded." I must say I have heard the expression before. It seems when it comes to religions, the Christian faith takes it on the chin more than others regarding this claim of exclusivity. But do not forget, all religions are not the same. All religions do not point to God. All religions do not say all religions are the same. At the heart of virtually every religion is an uncompromising commitment to a particular way of defining who God is or is not and, accordingly, of defining life's purpose. They may be superficially similar but fundamentally different, and many of them claim to be right and the others wrong. Indian culture has the appearance of openness, but it is highly critical of anything that hints to challenge it. It is no accident that within this so called tolerant culture was birthed the caste system, which assigns you to a particular status in life at life. And yet so many still blame or portray the poor little Christians as being unintelligent or elitist. It is with this thought in mind that I would like to speak to the exclusive claims of not only Christianity but a number of other religions.

You have probably heard some of the questions people pose about Christ's claims of exclusivity. Such as, "How dare you make such an audacious claim that there is only one way to heaven, God has obviously placed a piece of himself in all religions?" Some even say, "Is it not impossible to know with certainty which religion is true?" As a believer in Christ, I would counter by saying, "Why would God hide Himself in all the words religions?" Like some great scavenger hunt for God, you find a piece here and there. Hinduism alone has 330,000,000 different gods. If there is a God, why would He not make it plain? Some statements made by religious people are obviously false. I stated earlier, "Truth must coincide with fact and reality, and two mutually exclusive statements cannot be true." Therefore a religious philosophy that cannot meet the truth test must eliminate itself.

No other major religious figure made the claims that Jesus did. Various holy men claimed to have been sent by a higher power but did not claim to be that higher power. Neither Buddha nor The Prophet Mohamed claimed to be God. Jesus claimed to be God in the flesh. So in this regards Jesus is truly unique. Skeptics claim history is filled with stories of men and women from numerous cultures who claimed to be born of a virgin. So there is nothing unique about the assertion that Jesus was born of a virgin. One such example is story of the birth of the Egyptian god Horace (Heru), who was the son of Isis and Osiris. As the story goes Osiris was killed by his brother, Seth, who killed him and cut him into pieces. Isis, wife of Osiris, reassembled the pieces of her dead husband's body, but his original penis was missing. Isis then had another one made for Osiris in which she hovered over in the form of a hawk and became pregnant. Judge for yourself if you think that is immaculate.

The statements Jesus made concerning himself

are unique to him. Jesus said, I am the way, the truth and the life: no man cometh to the Father, except by me (John 14:6). Jesus was claiming to be God. He claimed to be able to forgive sins, an act reserved solely for God (Mark 2:10). The Jews even wanted to stone Jesus. Stating, you being a man have made yourself God (John 10:33). Now anyone can say anything at any time. Even when confronted about being able to forgive sins Jesus stated, what is easier to say thy sins be forgiven the, or take up thy bed and walk (Mathew 9:5). Not only did Jesus make exclusive statements but he backed them up with action. He said, destroy this temple and in three days I will raise it up (John 2:19). His statement was so astounding the chief priest and the Pharisees asked Pilate to put guards outside of his tomb after his death (Mathew 27:62). The Jewish religious leaders knew exactly what Jesus meant when He said, before Abraham was, I Am (John 8:58). Jesus was claiming to be God of all creation not a representative of some vague spiritual force.

Now in our modern society more people consider themselves to be spiritual. It is a relatively safe position to take, giving you the best of both worlds. You have the appearance of spirituality but no connection to any religious philosophy. Therefore, you avoid any harsh criticism or deep philosophical questions concerning your worldview. But saying you are spiritual proves nothing. It may in an unassuming way validate the existence of a creator. When a person says, "I am spiritual," a thousand questions flood my mind. For instance, "Where does your spiritual power come from, can it be known, and is it personal?" "How did it choose you and no one else to reveal itself to?" Vague spirituality answers nothing regarding the great challenges we as humans face, it also leaves every man to define right and wrong for himself. That thought alone should be deeply troubling considering man's history of violence. Certain groups consider killing and eating other people a spiritual experience. Now we see how potentially dangerous the concept of ill-defined spirituality can be, it lacks a proper foundation. Vague spirituality is the equivalent of trying to build a house on top of a hot air balloon.

The Christian faith teaches that Jesus was the

Word made flesh (John 1:1). God manifested in human form, Jesus is completely God and completely man at the same time. No other religious worldview creditably places the God of all creation so intimately in the lives of His creations. Proclaiming that God humbled Himself by taking on human flesh, subjecting Himself to all the desires and issues we as mortal men face (Hebrews 2:16) As Christ, God was tempted like you and me. This revelation means that He allowed Himself to be beaten, slapped and tortured to show us how much He loved us. He was willing to go through such suffering for people who despised Him. When Christians are criticized for being exclusive or elitist, we must give attention to the concept of the almighty God, possessor and creator of the whole universe humbly walking the dusty streets of Jerusalem interacting with his creations.

Jesus was God in the flesh but it did not mean he was not subject to the challenges of being human. Jesus was in all points tempted as you and me (Hebrews 4:15), but His temptations were greater because the stakes were so high. If I was being crucified, I would be powerless to stop it. Therefore, I would have to accept it. Jesus was God in the flesh, and He had access to unlimited power. When they come to arrest Jesus, Peter draws his sword and cut off a man's ear. Jesus heals the man's ear, saying, "**Are you not aware that I can call on My Father, and He will at once put at my disposal more than twelve legions of angels?** But how then would the Scriptures be fulfilled that say it must happen this way?" (Mathew 26:53). It took an even greater restraint for Jesus not to use His divine power. It is one thing to take abuse from someone bigger and stronger than you, but it is another thing to take it from someone you could beat to a pulp without barely lifting a finger.

The scriptures declare that the devil tempted Jesus three different ways on one occasion. The last and most important test was for Jesus to fall down and worship him. The devil offered Jesus all the Earthly pleasures He desired, if He would simply bow down and worship him. That is an interesting proposition. Why would Jesus, the Word made flesh, bow down to the being He created? We know Jesus refused saying, get the hence Satan, for it is written though shalt worship the Lord thy God and Him only shalt though serve (Mathew 4:10).

I wondered why Jesus did not tell the devil he could not give him all the earthly pleasures of the world, because the world did not belong to the devil. But sometimes what goes unsaid can be far more powerful than what is said. In a commercial, a man was strapped to a lie detector machine and his wife asked him, "Did he think her sister was prettier than she was?" He laughed nervously and ripped the electrodes off. I know that is a light hearted example, but I hope you get the point. Satan went on to explain why he could offer it, Saying to Jesus, "All this power will I give thee, and the glory of them; for that is delivered unto me; and to whomsoever I will give it" (Luke 4:5-8). The reason Jesus did not tell Satan he could not offer him all the earthly pleasure he desired, because Jesus knew dominion over all the earth had been given to Adam and Eve in the garden. When Adam disobeyed God, dominion over all the Earth went to Satan. So, it would appear Satan has the ability to bless people with material wealth, fortune and fame.

Some critics suggest there is a contradiction between the eternality of Jesus and His earthly birth. It is an old theological point of contention, and the main argument proposed by Arius, a priest of Alexandria Egypt who had been excommunicated from the Catholic Church for improper teachings concerning the faith. At the council of Nicaea Arius asserted, if the son was begotten of the father, then the son had a beginning. Before He (Jesus) was begotten, by the father he did not exist. Arius was in total error concerning the scriptures and the divinity of Jesus Christ. Skeptics also falsely assume that Emperor Constantine made Jesus divine at the council of Nicea as a means to control the people. Prior to the council of Nicaea there, was already an established belief among the followers of Jesus that He was divine—and they died for that belief. Christians had been tortured and murdered in Rome hundreds of years before Emperor Constantine came to power because they refused to denounce their faith in Jesus as the messiah. Even the Hebrew Tanak was already in existence. It is a fallacy that Constantine somehow changed the Jewish texts to fit his agenda. Constantine made an attempt to unify church doctrine establishing the Nicaean Creed:

> We believe in one God the Father Almighty, Maker of heaven and earth, and of all things visible and invisible. And in one Lord Jesus Christ, the only begotten Son of God, begotten of the Father before all worlds. God of God, light of light, very God of very God. Begotten, not made, being of one substance with the Father by whom all things were made. Who for us men, and for our salvation, came down from heaven, and was incarnate by the Holy Spirit of the Virgin Mary, and was made man. And was crucified also for us under Pontius Pilate. He suffered and was buried, and the third day He rose again according to the Scriptures, and ascended into heaven, and sitteth on the right hand of the Father. And He shall come again with glory to judge both the quick and the dead, whose kingdom shall have no end. And we believe in the Holy Spirit, the Lord and Giver of Life, who proceedeth from the Father, who with the Father and the Son together is worshipped and glorified, who spoke by the

prophets. And we believe in one holy catholic and apostolic Church. We acknowledge one baptism for the remission of sins. And we look for the resurrection of the dead, and the life of the world to come. Amen.

Scriptures declare, "In the beginning was the word and the word was with God and word was God" (John 1:1). Let us pause and examine this scripture as to how it relates to the eternality of Jesus Christ. If you do not understand how Jesus can have a physical birth and still be eternal. If I were at the Council of Nicaea I would have asked Arius, "Was there ever a time when God could not speak?" I posed this question to an adult Sunday school class one morning, and an older gentlemen shouted, "Never!" He was right of course. If you say yes, you are limiting God. If you say no, and you understand that Jesus is God, and you are affirming the eternality of Jesus. I must admit I thought this concept is revolutionary when it entered my mind, and I still do. It is with this thought I see how human Jesus can also be eternal God. I will take it a step further. Imagine if you are with someone and you tell them tell to bring you a glass of water and they do. Ask yourself did you get the water or did your word do it for you. That is the simple yet powerful truth of (John 1:1) when God spoke, Jesus the Word did it.

"All have sinned and come short of the glory of God" (Romans 3:23). After Adam and Eve sinned, all human beings were born into this fallen world filled with pain and suffering. Things were not as God originally intended (1 Corinthians 15:21-22). We can ot measure up to God's standard, so He came down to us. God has always been responsible for man, even his redemption. See, God is holy through and through, there is no evil in Him. We are sinners, sin means to have missed the mark. You may object to being called a sinner. If you are honest with yourself, you know there are things you think and say that let you know you are not *that* good. You may also question why you or I to suffer for something Adam did in the garden. I am reminded that nobody had to teach me how to lie, steal or disobey my parents. If nobody taught me how to do these things, there must be something in our nature that prompts us to do things we feel within ourselves are obviously wrong. That feeling alone should be some sort of indicator of a moral law at work within us.

Sometimes people raise the problem of pain. Asserting that God cannot possibly exist because the world is filled with so much pain and suffering. I believe in a world such as ours pain and suffering has its place. I had a surgical procedure done to repair a torn ligament which left my hand temporarily numb. I quickly realize how vulnerable my hand is to further damage, because I cannot feel its pain. It may sound strange, but I was glad when the medication wore off, and my hand could once again feel pain. I love a poem by Herbert Spencer called "The Pulley." One stanza states, "Let him be rich and weary, that at least. If goodness lead him not, yet weariness may toss him to my breast." It is at our most painful moments God wants us to know that He is near and loves us more than we will ever know. Jesus said, "I will not leave you comfortless: I will come to you" (John 14:18). He was letting us know he cares for us. In our pain we can go to him, you may be thinking. *What could God possibly know about pain? He does not have a clue as to how bad I am hurting.* That is when Jesus shows you His scars and says, "Look at my hands, look at my feet, look at my side. I went through all of this, so I could show you how much I love you. When you go to Jesus, you have the assurance that He knows and feels your pain. God allows His only Son to be tortured and executed on the cross. A punishment so heinous and gruesome that no Roman citizen can be crucified. Could God have done it another way? Maybe, but he felt it necessary to do it that way.

God's ways are past our understanding. In the scriptures when Jesus gets the word that Lazarus is sick, He purposely delays His arrival, and when He gets there Lazarus was dead. When Mary sees Him she said, "Lord if you had been here our brother would not have died." (John 11:21). She was right; Jesus had purposely delayed four days. But Jesus knew what he was about to do. He has a greater purpose for his actions: to teach Mary and Martha a tremendous lesson. Jesus is teaching them, "I am the resurrection, and the life: he that believes in me, though he was dead, yet shall he live." (John 11:25) Jesus is speaking of the authority over death and life given is given unto him because of His sacrifice. For as by one man's disobedience many were made sinners, so by the obedience of one shall many be made righteous (Romans 5:19). We could not measure up to Gods standard, so Jesus becomes the propitiation for our sins (1st John 2:2).

Isaiah 61:1-3 says, "I'll give you a crown of beauty for ashes". In order to have ashes something must have been burned up that was in existence. Some things we go through in life are so painful and traumatic only God can go through the fire with us. I may have the best intentions but the weight of your pain may be too great for me to bear. The fire will consume you both, but if you have God, you can go through the fire and not even smell like smoke. I do not know what you have gone through but God is able to heal your deepest hurts. God declares in Joel (2:25) I will restore unto you the years that the locust hath eaten, stressing His power to restore true happiness back into your life in spite of all you have been through, I must also reiterate this point, if there is no God you have no complaint; it is just life. Atheists will tell you is just too bad, but bad things happen in a world such as ours. Yet, Jesus Christ stands alone in His sacrifice, scriptures declare, But he was wounded for our transgressions, he was bruised for our iniquities: the chastisement of our peace was upon him; and with his stripes we are healed (Isaiah 53:5). Jesus dies for the redemption of the whole world, so in that since he is unique.

* * *

Shall not the Judge of all the earth do right?

– Genesis 18:25

Hell is where everyone is doing his own thing. Paradise is where everyone is doing Gods thing.

–Thomas Howard

The only place outside heaven where you can be perfectly safe from all the dangers and perturbations of love is hell.

– C.S. Lewis

CHAPTER 9
IS HELL JUST?

I am sure we have all heard someone curse another with, "Go to hell." The phrase is meant to be the ultimate put down and dismissal of your worth as a human being. It seems that hell is reserved for the worst of men. It is with this statement that I will address my next thought on how a loving God can send his prized creation to hell. A place described in the Bible as a realm of everlasting torment. Some may ask, "Why a loving God would even create such a place?" Would not its creation speak to the viciousness of His character? And if God is that cruel, why would I want to go to heaven to be with Him anyway? First of all, Scripture declares hell was not made for man, but it was made for the devil and the angels who sinned and rebelled against God's rule. (Mathew 5:41) I also think in order to give the thought of God throwing people into hell serious discussion, you must first ask yourself three questions. Is there a God at all? What does He require of me? And is hell just?

As you can imagine, I chose number one for the simple reason that if there is no God, nothing in life really matters anyway. Every man gets to define right and wrong for himself. There are no moral absolutes and everything is permissible. Now, as per number two, who is the right God among the many gods, and what does He require of me? Does He have any laws that I should be following? If I do not follow them, what are the consequences of my rejecting them and rejecting Him? Number three, is hell just in light of the pain and suffering we face in life? God had to have known beforehand what kind of world he was creating. If God did not know, he is stupid and if he did know, he is sadistic. One can argue, "God has obviously placed us in a perceived non-winnable situation. When you cannot live up to His standards, he says alright I am going to throw you into hell."

I know that the topic of hell and judgement can be a pretty sensitive subject. The notion of a loving God throwing His creation into a place of torment sounds cruel. Meanwhile, the ones whom He deems worthy of His affection get to go to heaven. Is that really just on God's part? It is a fair question. God's actions do seem to be unfair on the surface. Perhaps you think man should be free to live as he pleases without any accountability. Maybe you do not think you are that bad and hell seems like too severe of a punishment. After all, surely God cannot really be that unreasonable?

This is where I feel things get complicated, but follow me. Why do you feel God should let you be and not force his will on anyone? If that is your position, there is something you must also address. If you want God to leave you alone, what world would you live in? You may be asking right about now, "What are you talking about? I would live in this world." Your choice poses a problem because this world belongs to God, and He has made it perfectly clear that He is coming back to straighten it out to his original intent and spend eternity with the people who want to be with Him. While punishing those who have committed acts of injustice, if you feel you are not that bad and do not deserve to go to hell. God would have to create another world just for you and everyone else who feels the same way as you do. To live in an inhabited world, would require you to interact with other people. God has rules and laws to govern His creations and the people who will be inhabiting his new Earth want to live with God. You will be the odd man or woman out.

Before you get excited at the possibility of having your own world, you must consider what your world would be like. Would there be other people in your world? If so, will they have free will just like you, and if not, what sort of creatures would they be? It will be up to you to fashion your world and design it in any way you see fit, but here is the twist: you are using the imagination that God has given you. I once had an idea for a children's book. As I began creating my characters, it was proving to be more difficult than I imagined. I had to imagine what they looked like, their personalities, and the rules that governed their world? Even a fictional world has to have laws governing its existence. It is then I had a thought: how hard it must have been for God to develop and sustain all of creation. So, while you are designing your world, keep that thought in mind.

You alone are now responsible for designing your world and the fair treatment of everyone in it. What will you name your world? Let us be comical for a moment and call your world Marshmallow. What happens when your fellow Marshmallowians disagree with you or do not like you? Would you want them to love you, and to treat each other fairly? Now, I think we are really beginning to see how complicated it is becoming. The only remedy will be to put you on a world by yourself. To me, that will be a living hell, and you probably still will not be happy in your own world. I do not know about you but sometimes I get tired of me.

What if others in your world start to resent you? Would you stress that they should appreciate you more? What laws would you enact in your world? An even greater question, what would happen if the inhabitants of your world rebelled against you? I am sure you will be like, "How dare you! This is my world and I let you live here by my will." Now I believe we are beginning to get a glimpse into the heart of God and how He feels.

You see, on your world you will not be omnipotent, you still depend on God's power? Here is another dilemma. What will you say to God about the inhabitants on your world if you are displeased with their actions? So, even the perceived remedy of putting you on a world by yourself is flawed. The only logical conclusion will be to spend eternity with God or without him, He is the only one who can fulfill you personally. God alone is capable of making everyone who trusts in Him eternally happy. In your world, you cannot make yourself happy because your happiness depends on other outside factors and people.

This is where I think the Christian faith has an advantage over other religions. Remember God is a god of justice and mercy. The two have to be held at the same time, but God is ever ready to show mercy to us (Psalm 145:8). And there is an interesting theme of a redeemer who flows throughout the Bible. Who is this mysterious figure who is supposed to stand between God and man? If you follow the Scriptures, you know of this promised Messiah. He was none other than Jesus Christ Himself; the Scripture declare that the lamb was slain from the very foundation of the world (Revelations 13:8). That is an interesting thought. You might ask, "Do you mean to tell me that before God ever made man, He had already made plans to interject himself into suffering humanity?" It seems that this cruel and petty God is not as bad as his critics say. God was thinking about his creation before the earth was ever formed.

We must also consider the notion of free will. Your free will is the one thing God will not violate. If he does you are no longer free. You may even ask, "If God is all powerful, how I can be truly free?" The best way to answer is to tell you God is an eternal being, existing outside of time and space. The Scripture declares, whom He for knew He predestined to be transformed into the image of His son (Romans 8:29). God has the ability to look through time and has already seen your decisions. You are in essence totally free. If you have chosen to follow Jesus, and there is uncertainty in your life. God is working it out for your good (Romans 8:28). When you surrender to Him and say, "Not my will but thy will be done," You are giving him permission to guide you. I do not know about you, but there have been some things I thought I wanted. Yet when the opportunity to have them presented itself, I realized I did not want it after all.

Some years ago, I am looking for a career change. I think about driving semi-tractor trailers. I have a couple of cousins who drive for a living, so I ask them if I can tag along. To see what it might it might be like. After I completed runs with them, I got out of the truck and had the worst headache. I believe it was God's way of telling me, "This is not for you." After that realization. I had a conversation with my aunt who directs me the medical field. When I go to the college to inquire about the respiratory therapy program, it does not fit with my work schedule. The instructor then takes me to the director of the nursing program. She drops so many hints I would have been a fool not to apply. I apply, get in, and later pass my state board exams to become a licensed practical nurse. Everything falls into place, and I love my new profession. I feel God knew I am better suited for nursing than trucking.

Some may even ask why God can even create

such frail creatures. Well, ask yourself why do you choose to love some of the people you love? Some of them may not be good people at all, but you choose to love them anyway because they are your fellow human beings. Most people want to be loved. But the very thing that makes love possible is the thing that makes hatred possible: freewill. True love must be freely given, it cannot be forced. God can make a world filled with obedient drones but then there can be no true love. Sure, choosing to love someone can be scary, they may not love you in return. But we see that God is committed to loving His creations no matter the cost. Like one old preacher said, "God bankrupted Himself, He gave all he had." If it meant dying on a cross to pay the penalty for man's disobedience, so be it.

Let us look at it from this viewpoint. People, as human beings, know the horror and brutality other human beings are capable of. Yet, with this knowledge in mind, people continue to have children. Our existence speaks to that fact. It can seem that if we as human beings are willing to love and bring life into the world not knowing what contribution or horror they will add to society. How we can condemn God for choosing to create us. God gives us the gift of life, what we do with it is up to us.

I will take it a step further. We have no problem with locking someone up for life who has committed a horrific crime. It does not bother most of us the least that an individual will spend the rest of his natural life in a small concrete cell, only to be let for an hour a day for exercise if possible. Some people may say, "Why God would put people in hell? Why cannot He simply annihilate them?" He might make it as if they never lived. That way they will not suffer for all eternity. I find several problems with that argument. Once a thing exists, it impossible, even for God to make it as if it never existed. The Bible says God cannot lie (Numbers 23:13), if you asked Him a about someone you once knew He would give you an honest answer. What do you do with the people who knew someone who was annihilated? Do you wipe away everybody's memory? I think not. The effects of annihilating someone could be troubling to some. How can I truly have a relationship with God knowing if He desired He could simply wipe me from existence? On the surface, annihilating a person may not seem logical the more you think about it. Also, if a person who committed horrible crimes was just annihilated and wiped from memory. Was it just? They will be let off the hook, with no accountability for their actions.

Some might even say, "Why God does not give people more time to change?" I will counter by saying time does not change people who really do not want to. A million years will not be enough for some. If they do not change in a hundred years, what makes you think they will change in a thousand? If they are firm in their convictions not to want any part of God, He will not force them to be with Him. Since all of us are God's creations, He does watch over the world holding evil in check. He still has a responsibility to His creations. Some people have to be stopped by an outside power greater than themselves. It is true; if not they would rape, rob and steal all their days, so God steps in to stop the insanity.

Death is one intervention by God. Scripture

declares God limited man to a 120 years of life because his imagination was wicked all the day long (Genesis 6:3). In the beginning, it is not His will for us to die. The aging process is also a way of getting our attention. I do not care how you exercise and eat right, your body will still ultimately decay. I attend Sunday school one morning, and an elderly gentleman is talking about how much his wife trusts that he's being faithful to her. A sassy elderly lady sharply replied, "That's because its time out for you." It is quite funny looking at the expression on his face. She told me afterwards, "I couldn't let him get away with that, he knows he's too old and sickly to do anything." So try as you may to stay young, youth will not last.

The Christian faith teaches a resurrection of the dead and a judgment. The thought of a loving God causing His creation pain seems cruel, but we must also remember God created man with free will. So He is not going to force someone to spend eternity with Him. I recently watched a video of the late Christopher Hitchens as he expresses his disdain for God and his personal desire for not wanting to spend eternity with such a cruel and petty being. Talk about cruel and unusual punishment, to spend eternity with someone you loathe. When Adam and Eve sin, God cannot let them get away with it, because the wages of sin is death. If God overlooks their sin, the Devil can be the first one to say, "God you are an unjust hypocrite. How can you punish me and let them off?" Of course, the devil will be right. God cannot go against His own character and Adam and Eve choose to step out of the light of God's presence into the darkness of sin. Their actions had brought death upon them and the whole human race.

Let us explore that thought for a minute. Two of the attributes of God are love and light. In my humble opinion, it cannot take very much to see that without God you have darkness and hatred. I do not know if you have ever been in a place so dark you can feel it. Something about the darkness scares most people. Maybe the fear of uncertainty, you cannot even move or you may fall and hurt yourself. Sometimes sheer panic ensues, almost like the panic small child feels when they have wondered away from their parents. When we choose to step away from God by default, we are accepting the absence of light and love for all eternity. There is only darkness and hate. These characteristics definitely fit the entity called the devil, who will be cast into the lake of fire because he chose rebel against the Omnipotent God and cause men all the pain and suffering he possibly could.

The thought of hell is disturbing, but unfortunately it is necessary. True justice demands the existence of hell because God cannot allow evil to go unpunished. Not one tearful moment of suffering is unnoticed by God. God is just and no one gets a free pass to commit evil acts. It is no insignificant triviality to God that we are wondrous creations made in his image. And God loves us with an everlasting love. God also loves us enough not to violate our free will, if you do not want to spend eternity in His presence, He will not force you to. The Bible declares hell hath enlarged herself (Isaiah 5:14). Testifying to the fact that it is man's own wickedness brings the judgement of hell upon them, not God. The saddest day in the history of creation is when God is going to look down on his prized creation and pride and joy, telling them, "You have not chosen the sacrifice I provided for your redemption in my Son, Jesus Christ. In doing so you have chosen not to spend eternity with Me. Thy will be done.

* * *

Never be afraid to trust an unknown future to a known God.

– Corrie Ten Boom

I don't know how to live good. I only know how to suffer.

–Bob Marley

Talent is God given. Be humble. Fame is man-given. Be grateful. Conceit is self-given. Be careful.

–John Wooden

Chapter 10
My Two Cents

"My two cents" is an old but very familiar phrase. On the surface, it can be used with a statement you may make that someone is not obligated to accept. This chapter expresses my opinions and input on the subject of God, suffering and life. Make out of it what you will. I have presented arguments from others for the existence of God. Now I shall present my thoughts on God, and how I feel you as an individual are perfectly within your reasonable rights to maintain your belief in Him. Have the confidence to know God cares for you more than you will ever know, and the strength to tell those who are harshly criticizing you. That your decision to believe that Jesus was God in the flesh, is not haphazard or a delusion but is built upon a solid biblical foundation. Which has withstood centuries of intense examination.

Your search for the truth must be yours and it

cannot lie solely in the hands of other individuals. You must be willing to put in the time and investigate it the claims of Jesus Christ compared to other religious figures for yourself, and be willing to follow the evidence wherever it leads you. I will not tell you that I understand everything in the Bible, but I accept it based upon the entirety of the evidence. Some evidence in an investigation may not make sense by itself, but after putting it all together, you hope it leads to the truth. The Bible has proven itself trustworthy and reliable. I often hear people falsely assert that the Bible we have is a copy of copy, and therefore is unreliable. The Jewish historian Flavius Josephus stated, "We have given practical proof of our reverence for our own Scriptures. For although such long ages have now passed, no one has ventured either to add, or remove, or to alter a syllable; and it is an instinct with every Jew, from the day of his birth, to regard them as the decrees of God, to abide by them, and if need be, cheerfully to die for them."

Oddly enough, we are aided by history in our defense of the scriptures by the greatest unintentional discovery of Hebrew biblical text. It is by sheer coincidence that a shepherd is looking for his lost sheep and throws a rock into a cave near the Dead Sea, in hopes of scaring the lost sheep from its hiding place. When he heard the sound of pottery breaking. He entered the cave finding some scrolls in clay jars, unbeknownst to him, some were ancient biblical texts. Before 1947, the oldest complete Hebrew manuscript dates to around AD 900. With this discovery, we now have Old Testament manuscripts that have been dated by paleographers to around 125 BC. The Dead Sea Scrolls, as they are called, are a thousand years older than any previously known manuscript.

The book of Daniel, chapter 2, tells of Daniel's interpretation of the meaning of the statue in King Nebuchadnezzar's dream, which accurately portrayed the Babylonian, Medo-Persian, Greek and Roman empires. Then a goat "came from the west" (Daniel 8:5) with a single horn between its eyes. The horn represents the king, Alexander. The goat killed the ram and "became very great, but at the height of his power his large horn was broken off" (Daniel 8:8) – a prediction of Alexander's untimely death. In Daniel's vision, the single horn is replaced with four new horns, which are "four kingdoms that will emerge from his nation but will not have the same power" (Daniel 8:22). The four new kingdoms are mentioned again in Daniel 11:4, which says that "his [Alexander's] empire will be broken up and parceled out toward the four winds of heaven. It will not go to his descendants, nor will it have the power he exercised." These passages describe precisely what happened to Alexander and his empire. Some scholars, astounded at the accuracy of Daniel's prophecy, tried to post-date his writings even though historical and biblical factors point to a date of writing in sixth century B.C., well before Alexander's rise to power.

The Scriptures also foretell of the location (Micah 5:2), manner of birth (Isaiah 7:4), death and resurrection of Jesus Christ (Isaiah 53:5). Specific occurrences cannot be haphazardly dismissed, like the nation of Israel. How does this tiny nation against all odds continue to exist, and why do so many people consider it land the holiest place on earth? Observing all the turmoil in the Middle East prompts me to give extra attention to the Bible.

The Middle East can be unpredictable and has been ever since I was old enough to pay attention to it.

People deny the supernatural elements in the Bible, not acknowledging that the existence of the universe itself is supernatural. They do not think the natural laws that govern our universe can be violated. I do not believe these natural laws are actually being violated. God is the one who set the laws in motion, so He can suspend them at will. I see no contradiction in believing in the natural laws that govern our reality and an all-powerful God who can interact with his creations, while maintaining those laws. How can finite creatures such as ourselves possibly comprehend God– or fully grasp the how awesome he is?

What I am about to express neither proves nor disproves the existence of God. It is just the sharing of an event that profoundly changed me. In fact, I have wrestled within myself whether to even include it. But I have been honest and candid thus far, so I will not be true to myself if I exclude it. Some years ago, what I perceive to have been a supernatural experience occurs at church. It is in no ways meant to take the place of biblically sound doctrine. The scriptures are the ultimate authority for believers when it comes to descriptions of heaven and the afterlife. With that being said it was an ordinary day, nothing that can suggest anything otherwise. My brethren and I are at men's choir rehearsal. It was not a particularly large group, nine at the most. We were rehearsing. I am singing, and I must admit that I am not that good of a singer. I am not going to stir anyone into an altered state of euphoria, just an altered state of laughter maybe. As I am singing all of a sudden my heart began to race, and my breathing becomes erratic. The room begins to get bright; it is an amazing experience because my eyes are closed. I begin to question in my mind what is happening, I am afraid at first but there was a part of me that knows what it is. I take a deep breath and surrender to the moment.

That is a conscious act of my will; God does not violate our free will. The only way I can explain it to you, it was as if God was saying, "Come up here, I am going to take you out that temporal plane just for a moment." I mean, really, how you describe the indescribable? I retained my will and my consciousness. I am like Dorothy in the "Wizard of Oz," when she looked at Toto and said, "We're not in Kansas anymore." Skeptics can undoubtedly tell me I was suffering from some form of hallucination, but I disagree. I was fully aware of what is happening. Besides, skeptics having omnipotent knowledge in such matters makes them very thing they passionately denounce, a god.

As I mentioned, I surrender to the experience. Prior to this incident, I have been seeking God, asking him to show me if he was real. The Scriptures declare, if you seek me you will find me Mark 7:7). Although it is God who gives us the desire to know Him. Jesus said, no man can come to me except the father draws him (John 6:44). I am not saying everyone's belief in Christ should be based on a similar experience, without such a personal event, the evidence for Christ's death, burial and resurrection is sound. After what seems like a brief moment, I say within myself, "Okay God, I'm ready to come down now." It is then I feel myself reenter this temporal plane. Once I gather my thoughts, I notice some chairs were lying on the floor behind me.

I ask my friends who knocked over the chairs that are behind me, to which they reply, "You did." Evidently, I am jumping and shouting. I hear some noise during my experience, but I am not aware of what it was. In the book of 2 Corinthians 12:3, the apostle Paul talks about being caught up to the third heaven. Leading me to believe I was in the presence of God, beyond time and space, in a place where there are no limitations. As you can expect, such an experience can have a residual effect. The feeling or euphoria or however you want to put it lasted for several days after that. Perhaps, now you see my dilemma in sharing such an experience. As I stated, it cannot be scientifically verified. It can be confirmed, if you ask everyone who was there, they can verify that I was jumping and shouting and knocked over some chairs. It can also be confirmed that I told some people about it and shared it one day with my public speaking class in college; that is verifiable. So make out of it what you will; this is my two cents on the matter of God and the universe.

I must add I am not alone when it comes to people testifying of supernatural experiences. The stories are out there. One story about Colton Burpoe is told in the book *Heaven Is for Real,* which is also made into a movie. Colton dies and claims he went to heaven. He tells his parents things that he should not have known. His, like many others, are just personal testimonies not meant to be taken as gospel truth. It is up to you to judge the validity of their claims. My story is my story, and I accept all the criticism that comes from me telling my story. The scriptures declare that if all the works Jesus performed were written down, the world not have room for the books that would be written (John 21:25). I truly believe that whatever miracles Jesus performed in the presence of His disciple's and publicly were adequate. You may say that should have written down more, but I can counter and say most people would not believe them anyway; this I am confident of.

I heard an atheist speak on the foolishness of religion and value of science. If I were there, I would have liked to have asked him, "Are you married? If so, when you look into your wife's eyes is there anything special about her, or is she just a random grouping of cells meant to procreate a doomed species hurtling towards oblivion?" Now if that is his idea of romance, I wonder what his wife would think of that. Without God you are forced to reduce love to some chemical reactions happening in the brain. There is nothing a special about the person you love. If you want to use the word love, because love it is not a scientific.

I am not against science, though I do not believe in evolution. I believe in adaptation as Charles Darwin observed it. As mentioned, if human beings evolved over the course of billions of years from primates, where are the fossil remains of these transitional species? Up to this point, no complete missing link skeleton has ever been found; every so-called missing link has turned out to be a hoax. The best fossil evidence science can offer is the 3.2 million old collection of bones called Australopithecus, better known as Lucy. Which is not a complete skeleton, and not considered a missing link skeleton by many paleontologist. So, it is with this totality of evidence in mind and what I have observed in life that I feel confident enough to put my trust in the Jesus and prepare for my eternal destiny.

It can appear that this body, although marvelous, is a vessel to house the spirit. The scripture's declares that God formed man from the dust of the earth and breathed into him the breath of life (Genesis 2:7). Anyone who has been around someone who has died will understand what I am about to say. A person can be alive one moment and dead the next, leaving an empty shell. It can be amazing and disturbing. I have seen people at the point of death gasping for air when they die. It is as if the breath of life leaves their body. I do not believe it is that simple, that death is the final outcome. I mean the body is just lying there, but what happened to the rest of the person? Do they cease to exist or is there something else? The Bible declares that the breath of life goes back to the one who gave it. Yes, the spirit goes back to his Maker (Ecclesiastes 12:7), and the body goes back to the dust from whence it came.

Christianity for me is the only religion that offers a loving God who deserves our worship and adoration. You may ask, how I can say God should be worshiped and adored, when the world is filled with such pain and torment. I feel no other God took personal responsibility for the condition of the world. Yahweh is the only God among the numerous religions, who shared in the suffering of his creations. I cannot worship a God who intentionally created a world where His creations had to endure so much pain, with no explanations of why such conditions exist. Truly a God who would take pleasure in the suffering of His creations would be sadistic. We see that the God of the Bible showed how much He loved us by dying on the cross. God's display of unconditional love lets us know how committed He is to his creations.

It is good to know that Jesus is ever with us when storms arise in our lives. On one occasion Jesus was asleep on the boat during the storm and his disciples were afraid (Mark 4:37-39). Although he was on board with them, it still did not stop the storm from arising. But Jesus got up and rebuked the wind and the waves. It is at our lowest moments that I feel God's love is the strongest. Like the famous portrait of the footprints in the sand, when Jesus and a man were walking along the sea shore. The man asks Jesus, "Why at the worst moments in his life did he only see one set of footprints?" Jesus responded, "It was those moments that I carried you."

It gives me comfort knowing I do not serve an impersonal distant entity, but a God who is concerned about every aspect of my life. Jesus told His disciples in John 15:5, "I have called you friends." It is good to know that I am a friend of God. Jesus earned my respect and reverence by dying on the cross. God suffers with us not because He does not care but because of man's fallen condition. God loves us even when we do not return His love. In one display of affection Jesus laments over His people saying, "O Jerusalem, Jerusalem, thou that killest the prophets, and stonest them which are sent unto thee, how often would I have gathered thy children together, even as a hen gathereth her chickens under her wings, and you would not!" (Mathew 23:37) God is always there extending His loving hand of grace and mercy. God's love for us is the beauty of the gospel. As David said, thy gentleness has made me great (Psalms 18:35).

The choice is yours to seek the truth. There are a lot of things to occupy your mind and time, but I implore you to keep your wits about you. Learn to think for yourself. Your mind is an awesome thing, use it. I will impart to you something I read when I was younger and what I feel has kept me from a life of meaningless pursuits. The scriptures declare, there is no new thing under the sun (Ecclesiastes 1:9); whatever you propose has already been done. There is nothing truly new. Know this, the world abides forever, but you will not. King Solomon had indulged in every pleasure his heart could desire, but when it was all said and done. He was miserable because he had left God and no earthly pleasure can fill that void. So fix your compass morally sound, because if you do not, someone else will set it for you.

Life is short, and as I pen his book I keep that in mind. Demand your right to be heard, to be free to disagree. God has already placed everything you need to know about Him within the Bible, His Word to you and me. The Scriptures declare it is the glory of God to conceal a matter and the duty of kings to search it out (Proverbs 25:2). Search out for yourself who is the originator of life. Do not take the coward's way out, saying, "Well, I really do not know what is true." Helen Keller once stated, "People don't like to think because thinking demands that you come to conclusions, and conclusions are not always pleasant." Yes, thinking can be unpleasant, and coming to conclusions require actions, and actions require strength. Some people do not like to act because it requires too much. Acting on your conclusion can turn your world upside down, prompting you to leave jobs, people and places in order to reevaluate your circumstances. As a thinking man, I have had to make tough decisions. I left a job I hated but that was paying good money. Some well-meaning people advised me to stay, but the conclusion I reached regarding my future was that I no longer wanted to work that particular job. I was not sure how I was going to make it, or what I was going to do. I believe you cannot put a price tag on peace of mind, so I paid a price and took action.

Up to this point, I have resisted the urge to be overly religious, but in Jesus I find the greatest friend. When my eyes close for the last time on this temporal plane, this mortality shall put on immortality (1ˢᵗ Corinthians 15:54), and I will awaken with new eyes to behold a new world. Where Jesus and so many of my loved ones are waiting for me. So, no matter how uncertain the future maybe. I am not worried because I know the God, who if he desired could blow out the sun as if it were a birthday candle. Jesus said, "I am He who was dead and now I am alive" (Revelations 1:17-18). Jesus conquered death and the grave. He is the Alpha and Omega, the first and the last, the beginning and the end (Revelations 1:8). God started humanity on its course, although man strayed from it, God is going to one day wipe away all tears (Revelations 21:4). I will end this book where I started. Holding to my original view, that all life without God offers you and me is a beautiful death—and without God, it is not beautiful at all. Godspeed.

* * *

References

77 FAQs About God And The Bible by Josh and Sean McDowell

The Devils Delusion by David Berlinski

There Is A God by Anthony Flew

The God Delusion by Richard Dawkins

Hitler's Cross by Erwin W. Lutzer

The Case for Christ by Lee Strobel

Other quotes come from assorted lectures by Myles Munroe, Sam Harris, Ravi Zacharias, John Lennox, Christopher Hitchens, William Lain Craig and Stephen Hawkins

All scriptures are from the King James Version of the Bible